GREEK RHETORIC AND
LITERARY CRITICISM

BY

W. RHYS ROBERTS

Translator of "Aristotle's Rhetoric," Editor of
"Longinus on the Sublime"

70320

PA 3265

.R64 G

LONGMANS, GREEN AND CO.
55 FIFTH AVENUE
NEW YORK
1928

PREFACE

ARISTOTLE'S Art of Poetry *has already been treated of, by Professor
Lane Cooper, in this Series. The
more immediate subject of the present volume
is, therefore, the Art of Prose (and particularly
the Art of Public Speaking) as viewed, crit-
ically and constructively, by the Greeks. But
in no literature, and least of all in that of
Greece, can prose be studied and appraised
apart from verse. The Greeks rightly thought
that, even for the prosaic politician or lawyer,
there were no better models than some of the
speeches found in the* Iliad *and the* Odyssey.—
*Thus much by way of explanation, if a vast and
many-sided theme should seem to lack artistic
unity in this slight sketch of it.*

CONTENTS

[vii]

GREEK RHETORIC AND LITERARY CRITICISM

I. PLATO: ARISTOPHANES

WHENEVER the students in a modern university are urged to shun the 'rhetorical' spirit and to prize the 'academic' spirit, they are listening, perhaps unconsciously, to the ever-living voice of Plato. For in his Academy, the first of all universities, Plato sought after wisdom and justice, and spurned that power of persuasion at all costs which he held to be the aim of the ordinary 'rhetor,' or public speaker.

Nowhere in Plato's dialogues is there a more scathing indictment of unscrupulous oratory than in the *Gorgias*. The *Gorgias* was probably written within ten years of Socrates' death, that crime of the free Athenian people in which an orator, Lycon, had taken a leading part. In it Socrates, who foresees his own end, sets over against the arts of rhetorical persuasion the transcendent claims of truth and justice, and thus provides two great watchwords for Plato's newly-founded school of philosophy, which was designed to train statesmen and men of science for the making of a more ideal world.

The sophistical rhetoric attacked in the *Gorgias* is, with its fine language and fallacious arguments, no guide to truth, but is well fitted to delude the credulous and ignorant. It is an ' artificer of persuasion,' [1] which shrinks from no device of flattery, but panders to prejudice and tickles the palate with dainty, seductive words. Its worst side is seen not in the old sophist Gorgias nor in his young pupil Polus, who in studied elegance of style outvies his master, but in the ambitious and shameless man of the world Callicles, who finds in it a useful ally in securing his own selfish interests and in enforcing the theory that might is right. To Socrates rhetoric of this description implies a radically false aim in life; the true rule of life is not any ignoble pleasure but justice and goodness, and the ideal man will hold that to do wrong is a greater evil than to suffer wrong.

The Academy of Plato could have opened

with no higher or more truly religious aspirations than those found in the *Gorgias*, a work which may be regarded as the best introduction alike to his philosophy and to any modern study of that absolute morality which scorns merely personal desires and interests where conscience marks out a path of its own. For the growing mind of a lad or girl it has still, like the *Ethics* of Aristotle, the freshness possessed by the great perennial problems of life and duty when seen through the eyes of gifted pioneers. Nor can it be said that the ' rhetorical spirit ' has vanished from the earth, or that the influence of Plato is no longer needed to expose and ridicule it.

The *Phaedrus*, the other Platonic dialogue specially concerned with the merits of rhetoric, seems, alike in dramatic date and date of composition, to be later than the *Gorgias* and in certain important ways to supplement it. Not three sentences have been spoken in either work before a notable rhetorician is named — Gorgias, a Greek of Sicily, and (in the *Phaedrus*) Lysias, an Athenian but the son of a Syracusan. Whatever quarter of the Greek world they hail from, Lysias and all other orators, or writers on oratory, have short shrift in the *Phaedrus*, as in the *Gorgias*. Their speeches, and their pedantic rules and terminology, are mocked unmercifully by Socrates.[2] Thus far the two dialogues are in accord. But in the *Phaedrus* [3] Socrates traces the outlines of a higher rhetoric, one that reflects true knowledge, studies the processes of human reason and the varieties of human character, and is employed in the service of right and religion. Given such a rhetoric, the soul can be, in the best sense, 'won by arguments.' [4] The political uses of this higher rhetoric are glanced at later in the *Statesman*,[5] where the rhetorician is, for once, found in good company. It is doubtful, however, whether Plato ever overcame his rooted distrust of Greek rhetoric, or saw in it either a true art (since no true art could be based on mere probabilities) or a branch, however humble, of any philosophy worthy of the name. In the scheme of education for his Ideal Commonwealth it finds no place, nor is there any trustworthy evidence that he taught it systematically in the Academy. For good or for ill, neither Socrates nor Plato was the man to admire greatly a power that displayed itself at 'public meetings.' [6]

Nowhere in Plato is the connexion between

rhetoric and literary criticism — the art of speaking and the judgment of writing — more clearly seen than in the *Phaedrus*. The speech attributed to Lysias, and that composed by Socrates, are there taken as concrete illustrations of general principles. Though in regard to these two speeches his attitude is ironical, Plato has a profound belief in the superiority, for all speaking and writing, of true knowledge and sincere utterance to mere opinion and misleading statement, and of the inspiration of genius to the pedantries of technical manuals.[7] Another great conception in the *Phaedrus*[8] is that every discourse should be like a living thing, with body, head, and feet of its own, and with all its members adapted to one another and to the whole: a 'literary drive' — the compelling instinct of authorship — should make each speaker or writer shape the several parts of his discourse into the organic and vital unity of an artistic composition. The inspiring principle should be the love of ideal beauty — that love and that beauty which vivify the *Phaedrus* and lift its writer on the wings of his soaring eloquence. It is in the great myth of the charioteer and his two steeds, and in the enraptured glimpses of heavenly beauty which the human reason may attain and afterwards recall, that the dialogue reaches the height not only of its imaginative power but of its oratorical and literary expression, finding alike a great theme and a central point of union in that divine madness, that yearning after beauty, which men call love. The love of beauty sheds its light throughout the *Phaedrus,* which has the 'radiance' of the name it bears. There is in all Plato no dialogue of greater grace and loveliness than that in which Socrates makes his way along the Ilissus towards the plane-tree and, when the talk is over, prays to Pan and the other gods who haunt the spot tò give him beauty in his inmost soul.

And yet in the *Phaedrus* as elsewhere in Plato there is not only the recognition and the glow of literary beauty but a deep-seated distrust of it. In the *Laws,*[9] that little read but most modern work of his old age, as in the *Republic* of his prime, Plato (through the mouth of his ' Athenian Stranger') laments that poets seek to give pleasure, bad as well as good, to their hearers rather than to make them better men. From his Ideal Commonwealth he would for this reason expel even Homer the prince of poets; and lover of verse and writer

[8]

of verse though he himself was, he can [10] sacri-
legiously turn Homer's poetry into prose. In
his own later prose works the supposed claims
of scientific truth as well as of moral goodness
make his way of writing less beautiful and
more austere. But he remains among the
greatest of all authors; and one of the chief
debts owed by literary criticism to him and his
influence is that, through the standing paradox
presented by his own practice and theory, he
teaches men to value but not to over-value literature, and to remember that it comes second to
the supreme demands of life and truth. The
contradiction itself, as regards speaking as well
as writing, has been noted memorably by a
Roman orator and an English poet. Cicero [11]
makes Licinius Crassus say that he had read
the *Gorgias* with a Greek teacher at Athens,
and that what struck him most was that Plato,
while satirizing the orators, seemed himself to
be the greatest orator of them all. This is
true; and true pre-eminently of the speech in
which Socrates, hiding as so often his eloquence
under the veil of a fable, brings the *Gorgias* to
a close. That speech is, in language no less
than in theme, the still, solemn echo of another
and a juster world. So with Plato's ' Defence '

of Socrates, which, like the conclusion of the *Gorgias,* is at once great oratory and great literature. In both utterances the thoughts may well be those of Socrates,[12] but not the form. Socrates was no writer, except of a few simple verses in prison; and it is no mere verbal quibble to say that no man, however gifted, *speaks literature.* A younger contemporary of Cicero's, a Greek critic [13] resident at Rome, was right in asserting that the *Apology,* in the shape in which he knew it and we know it, has never 'seen even the doors of a law court or an assembly, but was written with another purpose': written, that is, by Plato himself, in order to vindicate the memory of Socrates before the courts of all time and all existence. Plato's greatest gift to literature is that *Republic* from which the poets are banished. Let his critic be Milton, that other poet and puritan, who bids him, a man of imagination all compact, recall the poets exiled from his airy commonwealth, lest he its founder be himself driven forth:

> *Iam iam poetas, urbis exules tuae,*
> *Revocabis, ipse fabulator maximus;*
> *Aut institutor ipse migrabis foras.*[14]

In the *Republic* Plato would censor not poetry only, but painting, sculpture, music, archi-
tecture. One of the many dangers he there
sees in the arts is that they may make a man
less manly. So deep-seated and many-sided
being his distrust of artistic beauty, we cannot
greatly wonder that none of his dialogues offers
a general view of literary or any other art. The
Greeks of the age which he portrays were perhaps too busy in the creation of beautiful things
to spend much time in criticism, theory, classification, and analysis. Their language did not,
in fact, distinguish between handicraft and
what we call 'fine' art. Both were, with them,
'technical.' The doctor, the carpenter, the
bard, the sculptor, and the Maker of the world
were alike 'workers for the people': artificers,
artisans, artists, all in one. This confusion, if
it be entirely a confusion, had its advantages,
just as it was no bad thing to take for granted
that all speech (λόγος, *logos*) is logical, all words
reasonable; or that 'beautiful' and 'noble'
can be denoted by one and the same term
(καλός, *kalos*). Failing a general survey, scattered indications of Plato's views on the nature
of art may be found not only in the *Republic*
and other great works, but in one of his short-

est dialogues. In the *Ion* [15] Socrates maintains that any true criticism of poetry demands a knowledge of poetry as a whole. For the appreciation even of so supreme a poet as Homer, it is necessary also to have studied poets who are not so good or who are actually bad. An inspired poet may inspire his interpreters, but an interpreter who has no knowledge of an art, and its guiding principles, cannot rightly estimate what that art says or does. In confirmation Socrates appeals to the analogy of the other arts: painting, sculpture, music. In the *Republic* art is something better than a set of rules; it is a subtle and pervading influence which keeps afar from the minds of ideal citizens whatsoever is ugly and therefore base, and is a breath of pure, fresh air from the healthful hills, bringing with it the beauty of reason.[16]

The eminent place which, notwithstanding the ban on the poets in the *Republic*, literature held in Plato's thoughts, is shown not only by his own care in composition[17] and by his great tributes to poetic inspiration,[18] but by his continual quotations from Greek writers. Plato is, indeed, among the first and greatest quoters. But his quotations rarely carry with them criticism that is purely literary. For detailed criticism of speakers and writers his favourite method is parody, and in this he is at one with Homer himself, and with the dramatic poets, Aristophanes especially. In the second part of the *Odyssey* there are occasional mock-heroic lines or passages, and later times produced set parodies of epic poetry in the *Battle of the Frogs and Mice,* and in the *Margites* or ' Booby.' Even the tragic poets and the orators will gird at one another's plots or style. But parody is the special province of comedy and satire from Epicharmus to Lucian. And Plato is, in his way, a writer of comedy. As a literary type, Plato's dialogues, particularly the *Symposium,* find their nearest poetic parallel in the comedies of Aristophanes,[19] to whose brilliant if one-sided criticism of literature a brief reference seems both to fall within the scope of this volume and to offer a broad and fitting conclusion to the present chapter. Plato shows the true spirit of comedy when he parodies Prodicus and Hippias in the *Protagoras,*[20] Polus in the *Gorgias,*[21] and Greek funeral orations in the *Menexenus.* But he is at his best when, in the *Symposium,*[22] he quizzes the mannered style of the tragic poet Agathon, successor of Euripides and imitator of Gorgias, with the same healthy humour that Aristophanes turns against the same Agathon in the *Thesmophoriazusae*. In Aristophanes and Plato, as among the Greeks generally, parody is no merely frivolous diversion, but is cultivated as a fine art. Not sparing the great and celebrated, but rather singling them out for attack, it reminds all men that admiration and reverence should be sane and temperate, that raillery is wholesome, that the salt of humour is an excellent antidote against corruption. The *Symposium* mingles jest with earnest, tragedy with comedy, and closes with the great conception of a fundamental unity in dramatic gifts: a conception such as few, if any, Greeks had ever formed and such as could in no age be formed by men who did not feel that literature, however great, is less than the many-sided life which it echoes. In the *Symposium* Plato pictures Aristophanes himself as a guest at the table of Agathon, who is celebrating his first victory in the contests of Athenian tragedians, and unites host and guest in a common defeat — at the hands of Socrates — before the *Banquet* closes; in the final scene of all Socrates, the unwearied talker, is victor over his former comic assailant and victor over even the tragic victor of the day.[23] At daybreak Socrates was, we are told, forcing his two remaining hearers to admit that skill in writing comedy and skill in writing tragedy go together, and that the artistic writer of tragedy is a writer of comedy also. To this they nodded their assent, under constraint and scarcely following the argument, and first of all Aristophanes fell asleep, and then, as day was dawning, Agathon the host. Socrates himself, having outwatched them, rose and departed; and after reaching the Lyceum he took a bath, and spent that day like any other, and when it was over went home towards evening to rest.

In this scene, so strangely full of imaginative truth, the chief interest for Plato manifestly lies in the final victory of Socrates as he issues forth to study the tragi-comedy of life in the streets of Athens, and to anticipate perhaps in his thoughts a time when a poet like our own Shakespeare, moving freely among all men, should prove himself not only a supreme artist in tragedy but a writer of comedy also. But to us to-day, as we look back and think of the *Apology,* the *Crito,* and above all the *Phaedo,* Plato himself seems a supreme artist at once in comedy and in tragedy. The *Symposium* is a comedy of comedies; the *Phaedo,* no less, is one of the greatest of all tragedies.

If from the *Symposium* we turn to Aristophanes in his comedies, we find that, looked at from our present point of view, he is one of the earliest and greatest of literary critics. It is true that, as a poet-critic, he confines his criticisms almost entirely to the poets.[24] But among these he refers by name to some forty or fifty, — one or two of them epic poets, a few lyric, a larger number writers of comedy, and a still larger number writers of tragedy. Familiarity is apt to blind the scholar to the number, variety, and brilliance — in words, metres, scenes — of the literary allusions, the parodies and travesties, found in all the plays of Aristophanes and pervading some of them from end to end; but we have only to turn our thoughts for a moment from the great wit of the ancient to the great wit of the modern world, and we see at once how vast a difference there is in this respect between Shakespeare and Aristophanes. We think of the play-scenes in *Hamlet* and in *A Midsummer-Night's Dream,* and of certain passages in *Love's Labour's Lost* and in *As You Like It.* We may recall, too, single lines which have all the appearance of parody, such as those of Falstaff in the First Part of *King Henry IV*:

Weep not, sweet queen; for trickling tears are vain;

and

For God's sake, lords, convey my tristful queen;
For tears do stop the flood-gates of her eyes.[25]

But on the whole there remains a striking contrast between the comparative rarity of literary allusion in the broadly human drama of Shakespeare and the amazing opulence of fancy and ingenuity shown in the parodies of Aristophanes.

Aristophanes is a great master of parody, and the more a master that he employs the art not as independent, but as ancillary to the art of comedy. Fun and entertainment are his chief aims, but with them goes keen literary insight, obscured sometimes by prejudice. He mentions, but does not waste time on, the new and worthless race of tragic poets, in the *Frogs;* the dithyrambic poet-impostors, in the *Birds;* the stale devices of the writers of comedy, in the *Wasps.*[26] His eye rests mainly on the great; to be repeatedly assailed by him may be regarded as an oblique compliment. We cannot reasonably expect a complete scheme of critical doctrine in a poet and a comic poet, but we are in little doubt as to the views, favourable or unfavourable, of Aristophanes concerning the poetic genius in general of (let us say) Aeschylus, and concerning Aeschylus' plots, characters, style, prologues, lyrics, stage appliances, gifts and powers as a teacher of civic virtue; we almost feel that he is anticipating Aristotle in the analysis, as given in the *Poetics*, of the elements of a tragedy. But whereas Aeschylus is credited by him with merits as well as defects, in the criticism of Euripides ridicule seems to reign everywhere and to leave little room for true appreciation.

There is no need to dwell on the skill with which, as the assailant of Euripides, Aristophanes makes his point. The point itself is, however, of peculiar and permanent interest in the history of literary art, and it may be illustrated almost as well from the less obvious and hackneyed case of Agathon as from that of Euripides himself. We have only to recall the words of Aristotle with reference to the *Flower*. 'In Agathon's *Flower* incidents and names alike are fictitious, and yet they give none the less pleasure. We must not, therefore, at all costs keep to the received legends, which are the usual subjects of Tragedy.' [27]   The words ' give none the less pleasure,' and ' at all costs ' mark excellently the contrast between the general attitude of Aristotle and that of Aristophanes — between the wise tolerance of the later philosopher and the fine intolerance of the contemporary artist.[28]

II. ARISTOTLE, *RHETORIC* I AND II — CONTEMPORARY AND EARLIER GREEK RHETORIC

THE points of contact between the *Rhetoric* and the *Phaedrus* are obvious and admitted; a word will be said about them later. The present writer believes that, in the first chapter of the *Rhetoric,* there are some little-noticed verbal echoes of the *Gorgias* which are meant as a direct challenge to the uncompromising denunciation of oratory in that dialogue. These echoes of Greek phrases are indicated in another publication.[1] The conclusion now suggested is that, when Aristotle came to include literature — poetry (the *Poetics*) and prose (the *Rhetoric*) — in his great survey of man's intellectual world, he wished to make clear his dissent from certain paradoxes which the *Republic* and the *Gorgias* had rendered famous. A city without poetry or oratory may be utopian, he seems to say, but it is hardly Athenian or human.

The first chapter of the *Rhetoric* forms a sort of Preface to the whole work. In this Preface Aristotle shows his usual good judgment when he says that the faculty of public speech must not be proscribed on the insufficient ground that it may be used unjustly; except virtue itself, all good things may be abused — strength, for instance, health, wealth. The great thing is to have truth and justice on your side, and to support them with the weapon of rational speech, which is the most distinctive attribute of man. ' Things that are true and things that are just have a natural tendency to prevail over their opposites, so that if the decisions of judges are not what they ought to be, the defeat must be due to the speakers themselves, and they must be blamed accordingly. . . . Again, it is absurd to hold that a man ought to be ashamed of being unable to defend himself by his limbs, but not of being unable to defend himself with speech or reason, when the use of rational speech is more distinctive of a human being than the use of his limbs. . . . Men have a natural instinct for what is true, and usually do arrive at the truth. . . . It is not right to pervert the juryman by moving him to anger or envy or pity — one might as well warp a carpenter's rule before using it. . . . We must be able to employ persuasion, just as strict reasoning can be employed, on opposite sides of a question, not in order that we may in practice employ it in both ways (for we must not make people believe what is wrong), but in order that we may see clearly what the facts are, and that, if another man argues unfairly, we on our part may be able to confute him.'[2] These prefatory warnings must constantly be borne in mind when, in the body of his work, Aristotle describes, without condemning, various artifices, subterfuges, and immoral sophistries.

Aristotle's formal definition of rhetoric comes at the beginning of his second chapter: ' Rhetoric may be defined as the faculty of observing in any given case the available means of persuasion.'[3]   *Speech,* as the organ of persuasion, is implied in the word ' rhetoric,' which means etymologically ' the art of the *rhetor,* — the speaker's (the public speaker's) art.' To make this clear, the Roman teacher of oratory Quintilian, when translating Aristotle's definition, inserts the word *speech,* — ' *rhetoricē* est vis inveniendi omnia *in oratione* persuasibilia '; for ' rhetoricē ' itself ' ars *dicendi* ' was a recognized Latin equivalent.   ' Art,' too, is implied in the formation of the Greek word; and Aristotle takes advantage of this fact to indicate that rhetoric is not only an art but a power or faculty — an ' art ' when regarded as a theory or system; a ' faculty ' when viewed in relation to the individuals who practise it. Further: rhetoric must ' observe ' (not quite ' find,' as Quintilian gives it) every available means of persuasion, however immoral; observe, but not necessarily employ. There is a fine sense of detachment about the Greek word θεωρεῖν (*theōrein*), with its large philosophical associations; and here we seem to be given early notice that Aristotle has in mind a *philosophy* of rhetoric, regarded as part of his encyclopaedia of knowledge. At the same time, the limitations of the art come out clearly in the last word of the definition. As the *Ethics* [4] reminds us, we do not demand scientific demonstration from the rhetorician, any more than we accept merely persuasive reasoning from the mathematician. Still, it is the argumentative (rather than the emotional) modes of persuasion that Aristotle stresses from the start. His very first words are, ' Rhetoric is the counterpart of Dialectic '; or, in other words, there is a close, though not an exact, correspondence between the art of pub-

lic speaking and the art of logical discussion.
'Persuasion is,' he says, 'a sort of demonstration, since we are most fully persuaded when we
consider a thing to have been demonstrated.
The orator's demonstration is the enthymeme,
and this is, in general, the most effective of the
modes of persuasion. The enthymeme is a sort
of syllogism.' [5] It is a syllogism based on those
probabilities which may be 'the very guide of
life,' but are nevertheless no more than probable and contingent. In Aristotle's own technical language, the premisses of the enthymeme
are either (1) 'likelihoods,' or (2) 'signs'; that
is, either (1) causes that are likely, but not certain, to produce a particular effect, or (2) effects
that may have been produced by a particular
action, which is possible, though not a necessary, cause of such effects. Blood upon a man's
clothes *may* be a sign that he has murdered another man; that he bore him a grudge *may*
make it likely that he has murdered him. Another form of rhetorical argument recognized
by Aristotle is the 'example,' or parallel case.
For instance, a speaker may wish to prove that
Dionysius, in asking for a bodyguard, is schem-
ing to make himself a despot, and may quote
the case of Peisistratus at Athens, Theagenes

at Megara, and any other cases known to him of the demand for a bodyguard being a preliminary to the establishment of a despotism. The process forms an induction, but not a conclusive induction, unless the list of precedents is at once complete and completely analogous. The example is, in fact, a rhetorical induction, as the enthymeme is a rhetorical syllogism. Rhetoric itself has regard to classes of men, not to individual men; its subjects, and the premisses from which it argues, are in the main such as present alternative possibilities in the sphere of human action and are not peculiar to any special science, and it must adapt itself to an audience of untrained thinkers who cannot follow a long chain of reasoning.[6]

Besides his power of proving a truth, or an apparent truth, by means of persuasive arguments, a speaker must also be able to suggest a personal character which will make his speech credible, and to stir the emotions of his hearers. It thus appears that rhetoric is an offshoot not only of dialectic but also of ethical studies. 'Ethical studies may' (to continue Aristotle's [7] account) 'fairly be called political; and for this reason rhetoric masquerades as political science, and the professors of it as

[25]

political experts — sometimes from want of education, sometimes from ostentation, sometimes owing to other human failings. As a matter of fact, it is a branch of dialectic and similar to it, as was said at the outset. Neither rhetoric nor dialectic is the scientific study of any one separate subject: both are faculties for providing arguments.' Or, as he says further on,[8] ' rhetoric is a combination of the science of logic and of the ethical branch of politics; and it is partly like dialectic, partly like sophistical reasoning. But the more we try to make either dialectic or rhetoric not, what they really are, practical faculties, but sciences, the more we shall inadvertently be destroying their true nature; for we shall be re-fashioning them and shall be passing into the region of sciences dealing with definite subjects rather than simply with words and forms of reasoning.' It should be added that Aristotle regards (1) the speaker's arguments, (2) the influence of his character when exhibited in his speech, and (3) his power of working on the characters and emotions of his audience, as belonging strictly to the *art* of rhetoric. Outside the art in its strict sense, fall those means of persuasion which he does not bring with him but finds ready to his hand: laws, witnesses, and the like.

Aristotle distinguishes three kinds of rhetoric: A. Political (deliberative), B. Forensic (legal), and C. Epideictic (the ceremonial oratory of display; *occasional* oratory). Their (a) divisions, (b) times, and (c) ends are as follows: A. Political (a) exhortation and dehortation, (b) future, (c) expediency and inexpediency; B. Forensic (a) accusation and defence, (b) past, (c) justice and injustice; C. Epideictic (a) praise and censure, (b) present, (c) honour and dishonour. The letters inserted here for the sake of greater clearness are not found in Aristotle himself, but together with many other similar modern devices they would have been used by him if they had been customary in his day; they are in keeping with his keen, orderly, logical, analytical mind.[9]

The subjects of Political Oratory are grouped under five main heads: (1) ways and means, (2) war and peace, (3) national defence, (4) imports and exports, (5) legislation. Each of these important subjects is discussed by Aristotle, briefly but with a sagacity which is astonishing. The political speaker must know how to appeal to his hearers' desire for happiness and for 'good' things; and this leads Aristotle to consider, in the popular way appropriate and usual in the *Rhetoric*, what constitutes happiness, and what is reckoned 'good,' positively and comparatively. The political speaker will find his powers of persuasion most of all enhanced by a knowledge of the four sorts of government — democracy, oligarchy, aristocracy, monarchy, and their characteristic customs, institutions, and interests. Each of the four varieties is defined, and its ends indicated.[10]

The Epideictic speaker is taken next. His concern is virtue and vice; the one he praises, the other he censures. It is necessary, therefore, to inquire into the various forms which virtue takes — justice, courage, temperance, magnificence, magnanimity, liberality, gentleness, prudence, wisdom; and to ask which are the greatest virtues.[11]

The Forensic speaker should have studied wrong-doing — its motives, perpetrators, and victims. Wrong-doing is defined as injury voluntarily inflicted contrary to law. There are seven causes of human action, viz., three involuntary, (1) chance, (2) nature, (3) compulsion; and four voluntary, viz., (4) habit, (5) reasoning, (6) anger, (7) appetite. All voluntary actions are good or apparently good, pleasant or apparently pleasant. Pleasure is accordingly defined, and things pleasant are analyzed. Actions just and unjust are also classified in relation to (1) the law, whether special or universal, (2) the persons affected, whether the individual or the State. Unwritten, as distinguished from written, law (1) includes in its purview the conduct that springs from exceptional goodness or badness, e.g., our behaviour towards benefactors and friends; (2) makes up for the defects in a community's written code of law. This second kind is equity; and its nature and scope are considered. Book I concludes with an account of the ' non-technical ' (extrinsic) means of persuasion, — laws, witnesses, etc.[12]

The contents of Book II can be more briefly sketched. Since rhetoric — political and forensic rhetoric, at any rate — seeks to effect decisions, the orator must not only try to render the argument of his speech demonstrative and worthy of belief; he must also (1) make his own character look right and (2) put his hearers, who are to decide, into the right frame of mind. In regard to his own character, he should make his audience feel that he possesses prudence, virtue, and goodwill. This is especially important in a deliberative assembly. In the law courts, it is especially important that he should be able to influence the emotions, or moral affections, of the jury who try the case. In regard to each emotion we must consider (a) the states of mind in which it is felt; (b) the people towards whom it is felt; (c) the grounds on which it is felt.[13] From these three points of view the following emotions are examined and defined: anger, calmness; friendship, enmity; fear, confidence; shame, shamelessness; kindness, unkindness; pity; indignation; envy; emulation.[14] The various types of human character are next considered, in relation to the various emotions and moral qualities and to the various ages and fortunes. By 'ages' are meant youth, the prime of life, and old age; by 'fortunes' are meant good birth, wealth, power, and their opposites. The youthful type of character is thereupon depicted; after that, the character of elderly men; lastly, the character of men in their prime, with the remark that the body is in its prime from thirty to five-and-thirty, the mind about forty-nine (Aristotle's approximate age at the time he was writing).[15] Next are described the gifts of fortune by which human character is affected; good birth, wealth, power.[16] In the remainder of this book, Aristotle deals more fully with those logical aspects of rhetoric which had been introduced in the first book and are always before his mind, and he enumerates as many as twenty-eight topics (lines of argument) on which enthymemes, demonstrative and refutative, can be based. He concludes with the statement that the account of the *thought*-element — the way to invent and refute arguments — is now complete, and that it remains to discuss style and arrangement.[17] It is likely that book III was issued later than books I and II, and in the present volume it will be convenient to make such a break and, before dealing with book III, to speak further of the first two books, and, in connexion with them, to touch on the general affinities and associations of the *Rhetoric*, in its relation to the history of the art in Greek-speaking lands.

Some remarkable sayings have already been quoted from the ' Preface ' to the *Rhetoric*. If space permitted, the great range, power, and penetration of the work might be further shown by citing from books I and II a few of those incidental remarks and miscellaneous illustra-

tions which seem to drop with careless ease
from Aristotle's unfailing store of thought and
observation: references to some slightly longer
passages of the same arresting kind are given in
the notes.[18]

The only direct allusion to the *Phaedrus* in
the *Rhetoric* comes at the end of book III, c. 7.
But it is possible that, at the every opening of
his treatise, Aristotle wishes to indicate a debt
to Plato as well as some dissent from him, and
that we may take his real meaning to be ' Plato
was wrong when, in the *Gorgias,* he caricatured
rhetoric as mere cookery and flattery and gave
it up as past redemption. But he was right
when, in the *Phaedrus,* he showed that it might
be reconstructed on the basis of reasoning and
psychology; and I lose no time in signify-
ing, through six words of obvious challenge,
that I mean, in the treatise now opening, to follow and go beyond the view sketched in the
Phaedrus and to treat rhetoric as a true art, and
not as a palate-tickling knack.[19] Let men like
Gorgias regard it as an ' artificer of persuasion ': [20] ' philosophers should be able to frame
a better theory of public speech, the power (to
wit) of observing in any given case the available means of persuasion.' On this foundation

Aristotle constructs, in place of Plato's hints, a great and systematic treatise. Notwithstanding the popular and variable character of the subject with which it deals, the *Rhetoric* is made to form part of a coherent and comprehensive philosophical system resting ultimately on a logical basis.

As a practical philosopher, Aristotle recognized, more clearly than Plato could bring himself to do, the importance of rhetoric, or the art of public speaking, as an instrument of popular government. He speaks of its great 'growth and advancement,' alike in the *Sophistic Elenchi* and the *Politics*.[21] In the *Ethics*[22] he ranks strategy, economics, and rhetoric among the 'most highly esteemed of capacities.' The *Ethics* itself is not explicitly mentioned in the *Rhetoric*, where, however, it is clear that Aristotle's own ethical system (though possibly not yet embodied in the *Ethics*) is already settled in his mind and that he is, for the moment, presenting a popular and less scientific exposition of it. The *Politics* is referred to once only, whereas the logical treatises and the *Art of Poetry* are cited several times. But quoted or not, the doctrines of both the *Politics* and the *Ethics* underlie the *Rhetoric*, especially in

books I and II respectively. In the *Rhetoric*
Aristotle is not greatly given to self-quotation.
Of the many rhetorical works attributed to
him, the *Theodectea* alone is named.[23] Though
he alludes incidentally to other writers on rhetoric, he never mentions his own ' Collection
of the Arts,' in which all the many pre-existing
' arts,' or handbooks of rhetoric, were included
with the same assiduity which we know him to
have shown in other investigations. Aristotle,
here as elsewhere, is true to his usual sound historical method of inquiry: a point in which he
excels Plato. As in his *Metaphysics*, where the
First Book gives a short sketch of Early Greek
Philosophy, as in the *Politics*, where alike tradition and the luckily recovered ' Constitution
of Athens ' attest his respect for the past, so
here he takes all due account of previous ef-
forts and experience. His ' Synagogue (Con-
gregation, Collection) of the Arts ' has been
lost, but his repeated references either to ' the
present-day writers on rhetoric ' generally, or
to specified teachers and theorists, are enough
to show that he has faithfully reviewed the
rhetorical field of his own and previous days.
And in the light of current shortcomings he
lays down the true philosophical principles of

rhetoric, considered as a branch of the science of man, and writes a treatise which has never been superseded and is never likely to be superseded. The *Rhetoric* has been described as an 'isolated' work. Its true distinction is that it does not stand alone without predecessors or successors, but that it stands apart and pre-eminent even where the predecessors and successors are so numerous; it is the most philosophical (or, scientific) work ever composed on the subject.

It is important to note how and when the formal study of oratory, as distinguished from the practice (as in the Homeric poems) of natural eloquence, originated. Nearly a century and a half before Aristotle's time, various despotic rulers were overthrown in the Greek cities of Sicily, and popular government was re-established. For civic and legal business, and particularly for the recovery of confiscated property, a class of trained speakers, learned in the law, was found useful, and the first treatise on rhetoric was written by a certain Corax, and the second by his pupil Tisias. The present writer thinks that Doric fragments or echoes of this rhetorical teaching can be read in the third volume of the *Oxyrhynchus Papyri*.[24] These early Sicilian advocates seem to have aimed at a simple, unstudied style, especially when opening their speeches; and also to have paid much attention to the orderly divisions of a speech, from proem to peroration. The arguments they favoured were those resting on probability or presumption, and they applied them sometimes in the quibbling dilemma-ridden spirit illustrated by the well-known story of the dispute between Corax and Tisias as to whether the former had earned his fee as teacher.[25] In the first chapter of the *Rhetoric*, Aristotle remarks that political oratory is less given to unscrupulous practices than forensic, because it treats of wider issues; and Plato, in the *Theaetetus*, has drawn an immortal picture of the narrowness of the lawyer; he is the world's slave, while the philosopher is the true freeman.[26] Still, we do well to remind ourselves that, in Greek Sicily as in other lands and ages, the lawyers were (like Plato himself) no friends of tyranny, and that in modern times some of the greatest of national ministers have been those who were at once lawyers and statesmen.

There was another side to the Sicilian rhetoric: one that was more literary than legal. Diogenes Laertius [27] tells us, on the authority of Aristotelian writings now lost, that Aristotle regarded Empedocles of Agrigentum as the 'inventor' of rhetoric. From the context in Diogenes, it is clear that Aristotle is thinking of those literary artifices, such as the use of metaphor, which Empedocles, in his public speeches, copied from Homer; he has in view not the subject-matter of Empedocles, but the form in which it is presented. In this respect, Empedocles was followed closely by his pupil Gorgias of Leontini, whose style possesses marked points of contact not only with the surviving fragments of Empedocles' poems, but with the poems of Homer and also of the three Athenian tragedians (Sophocles especially), with whom the long-lived Gorgias was wholly or in part contemporary. The poetical colour of Gorgias' style is commented on adversely by Aristotle: 'Now it was because poets seemed to win fame through their fine language when their thoughts were simple enough, that the language of oratorical prose at first took a poetical colour, for example, that of Gorgias. Even now most uneducated people think that poetical language makes the finest discourses. That is not true: the language of prose is distinct from that of poetry.' [28] Or, as a later

Greek critic puts it, ' Gorgias introduced poetical style into public speeches, not deeming it
right that an orator should resemble ordinary
people.' [29]   Thus Gorgias may be regarded as
the initiator of *epideictic* oratory, the oratory
of display and ceremonial, which took its cue
from the public recitations of Homer's poems.[30]
A later Sicilian, Diodorus, who lived in the time
of Julius Caesar and Augustus, has, in his *Historical Library*,[31] drawn a vivid picture of the
impression made at Athens by the oratory of
Gorgias when, in the year 427 B.C., he came
there on an embassy from his native city, Leontini.   Gorgias was then in the maturity of
powers that had probably been developed by
Tisias as well as Empedocles, and we are told
that he dazzled the clever, speech-loving Athenians by his distinguished and almost foreign
style.   He uses, Diodorus goes on, in uncom-
mon and elaborate ways, such shapes of language as antithesis (the elaborately antithetic,
or ' contrasted,' form of the sentence was one of
Gorgias' great points), rhyming terminations,[32]
and clauses equal in length and similar in structure.   At the time, the historian concludes, such
devices were welcomed owing to the novelty of
their craftsmanship, whereas now they seem

[38]

affected and ridiculous to ears sated by their
repeated use. Diodorus' characterization is
amply confirmed by a surviving fragment of
Gorgias' *Funeral Speech,* in which those pecul-
iarities which are attributed to his style in
general are clearly seen.[33]

The style of Gorgias was, in fact, what we
to-day might call 'euphuistic,'—a word which
is part of the long tale of Greek literary influence in English-speaking countries. The
word εὐφυής, *euphues* ('clever,' 'naturally
gifted'), used by Diodorus to describe the
Athenians who so eagerly admired and copied
Gorgias, is the very word which John Lyly,
with more knowledge of Roger Ascham's
Schoolmaster than of Diodorus, chose as the
title of two books (*Euphues, or the Anatomy
of Wit* and *Euphues and his England*), which
in the age of Shakespeare were almost as influential as the speeches of Gorgias in the days of
Thucydides. The euphuistic style seems to be
parodied when Falstaff enacts the part of King
Henry the Fourth and says to Prince Hal,
'Harry, I do not only marvel where thou spend-
est thy time, but also how thou art accompanied; for though the camomile, the more it
is trodden on the faster is grows, yet youth, the

more it is wasted the sooner it wears.' [34] Examples more extravagant than this were constantly on the lips of Queen Elizabeth, for Lyly addressed his books especially to women and the Court. Some of Gorgias' excesses are noted by Aristotle; [35] but his affectations and jingles are, as with Lyly, the faults of a man who was a great force in the development of artistic prose style, and that because he regarded prose as an art worth pursuing for its own sake and not simply as a means of expression: *la parole pour la parole.*

Gorgias was not only a rhetorician but a 'sophist.' It is not necessary here to discuss the character of the sophists as a class — how far they resembled modern journalists and professors. Certainly they cannot be condemned in a body, on the strength of the bad sense that 'sophist' and 'sophistical' bear to-day. Towards the end of the *Gorgias*,[36] Socrates says to Callicles, 'Sophist and rhetorician, my dear fellow, are the same thing, or as nearly as possible alike.' There is earnest beneath the pleasantry. To Plato's mind, at any rate, rhetoric, regarded as 'the artificer of persuasion,' was ready to accept any fallacious arguments from the sophist, while the sophist would accept all allurements of language from the rhetorician; and such rhetoric was not the ally, but the enemy of truth. The acceptance of a fee for their teaching was enough to condemn rhetorician and sophist alike in his eyes; and here he had Greek feeling with him. Xenophon in the *Memorabilia* [37] says that men who sell their wisdom to all and sundry for money have the opprobrious name of 'sophist'; and in the *Anabasis* [37] he tells how the high-minded young Boeotian Proxenus, in his desire to be trained for great affairs, 'gave money to Gorgias of Leontini.' Consequently we are not surprised to find Aristotle, at a later time when Gorgias and the other famous sophists had long been dead, framing this formal definition: 'a sophist is a man who makes money through the false appearance of wisdom.' [38] With this disparaging sense of the word in mind, he suggests [39] the useful distinction which we still observe when we speak of *'sophistical rhetoric,'* as opposed to the better kind of rhetoric which he himself taught. He implies that there is no special Greek term to denote the sophistical rhetorician, whereas the sophistical dialectician has the name of 'sophist.' 'Rhetor,' in fact, can mean either a *trained speaker* or a *tricky*

speaker: hence the equivocal meaning borne by
' rhetoric ' in all later times, the honest rhetorician having, to this day, no separate name
to mark him off from the dishonest.

The sophistical rhetoric is exemplified in the
so-called *Rhetorica ad Alexandrum,* once attributed to Aristotle and still printed among his
works.[40]   As it stands, the *Rhetoric to Alexander* cannot have been written by Aristotle, who
never mentions it, and none of whose works are
mentioned by it, though it refers (in its Intro-
ductory Letter, at any rate) to Alexander, who
was Aristotle's pupil but is never named in any
undisputed work of the philosopher.   Its
author may possibly be the rhetorician and historian Anaximenes of Lampsacus, a contemporary of Aristotle and Alexander.   It was
probably written not long after 340 B.C., the
date of the latest event recorded in it.   Fragments of it are preserved in the Hibeh Papyrus,
discovered in our own times and written probably between 285 and 250 B.C.; if these remains had included its opening pages, the question of authorship would no doubt have been
settled.   By whomsoever composed, the treatise, prolix and wearisome though it is for all
its brevity, is of the utmost importance as be-

ing the sole surviving representative of the current fourth-century rhetoric (reflecting the general theory and practice of a long line of rhetoricians from Corax to Isocrates) which, in his final and authoritative work on the subject, Aristotle took as his basis, while fortifying and re-fashioning it out of his logical and philosophical armoury and breathing into it a more truth-loving spirit than was usually found in it. This difference in spirit may be illustrated by a sophistical and immoral sentence from the *Rhetoric to Alexander*, one which surely has no counterpart in Aristotle's *Rhetoric:* 'This then (a deceptive method just described) is the way in which we shall treat evidence, when it is to our advantage to disguise it. If our opponents try to do anything of this kind, we shall expose their wickedness and order them to give their evidence in writing.' [41]

Among the actual writers of rhetorical handbooks we cannot with certainty class Isocrates, or his Sicilian predecessors Gorgias and Empedocles. These three remarkable men cover a long stretch of time: particularly Isocrates, whose life lasted through three generations, from 436 B.C., five years before the outbreak of the Peloponnesian War, to 338, the year in which the battle of Chaeroneia brought Greek freedom to an end. But many rhetorical precepts are to be found in Isocrates' extant writings or in fragments of his lost writings. These precepts, and the characteristics of his own style, can best be mentioned, as can the Attic orators generally, in the chapter which deals with Dionysius of Halicarnassus. Here we may glance at a few aspects of his personality, and at his probable relations with Plàto and Aristotle.

In the *Panathenaicus*,[42] Isocrates seems, at the age of 94, to be challenging the lofty paradox of the *Gorgias* and the *Republic* when he says that to do wrong rather than to suffer wrong would be the deliberate choice of 'all sensible persons, though some few of those who pretend to be wise might deny it.' In the *Philippus*[43] there is a reference to 'the laws and the polities written by the sophists,' meaning apparently Plato's *Laws* and *Republic*. Further: in more than one passage,[44] opinion seems to be exalted above knowledge, in direct opposition to Plato's teaching. On the other side, Plato has his say about Isocrates, in the *Gorgias*, when he represents rhetoric as the pursuit of a mind ' good at guesswork,' [45] and in the *Euthydemus*,[46] where he disparages the sort of man who is a bad blend of the philosopher and the politician and inferior to either, adding, however, magnanimously, that we must hold in esteem any and every man who says aught that approaches wisdom and manfully keeps to his purpose and toils away. This magnanimity appears again in a well-known passage near the end of the *Phaedrus*.[47] Plato had no petty desire to deny to Isocrates such philosophy, or ' love of wisdom,' as might be shown in intellectual activities generally; but his own pre-eminence, and that of Aristotle, in the unfettered search for truth made it inevitable that, from their time onwards, a clear line should be drawn between philosophers and rhetoricians, and that Isocrates should find his fitting place among the latter. It must, however, be admitted that Isocrates had, as Plato no doubt saw, a broad Hellenic outlook, and also that he could draw an attractive picture of various virtues which should distinguish the ' educated man.' [48] It is regrettable that this picture should be followed immediately by a fling, in Isocrates' petulant way, at those who ' recite in the Lyceum ' the poetry of Homer and Hesiod and ' talk twaddle ' about them.[49]   During his first residence at Athens, Aristotle seems to have set up a school of rhetoric, in opposition to that of Isocrates and with a more philosophical and truly literary background.   On Aristotle's return to Athens in 335 B.C., Isocrates was dead, and it is pleasant to see how often illustrations of good rhetorical practice are borrowed from his discourses for use in the *Rhetoric,* which seems to belong to that final period in Aristotle's career.   From Demosthenes, on the other hand, hardly anything is quoted, although he was Aristotle's contemporary in the fullest measure.   The reason may be that not many of Demosthenes' speeches were accessible in writing, or possibly that Macedonian prejudices had to be respected.   The mention [50] of Demosthenes' comparison of the Athenian people to sea-sick voyagers may rest on common knowledge, not on any publication.   As an illustration of the *post hoc propter hoc* fallacy, it is good to read: " Thus Demades said that the policy of Demosthenes was the cause of all the mischief, ' for after it the war occurred.' " [51] Aristotle had had close relations with Macedonian kings, but he was just and large-minded.

As compared with philosophy proper, Aristotle could not greatly value rhetoric, but he was careful to train his pupils in so necessary an art.[52] Some of the later Greek authors use an expressive word, one which has none but favourable associations, to describe his aims. Strabo[53] says that Aristotle, while making all his pupils 'good at speech,' made Theophrastus a 'master of speech.' Plutarch,[54] in a significant context, describes Aristotle himself as a 'master of speech.' Philip, he says, had observed that, however refractory the young Alexander might be, he could easily be led by speech (by λόγος, *logos,* or rational argument) to do what was right; and this was why he 'sent for Aristotle, the most famous of philosophers and a master of speech.'

III. ARISTOTLE, *RHETORIC* III—
DEMETRIUS ON STYLE

IN Book III of the *Rhetoric*, the main subject is λέξις, *lexis* ('style'), followed by a shorter section on τάξις, taxis (the 'arrangement' of the parts of a speech). Near the beginning of the book, Aristotle writes: 'Our next subject will be the style of expression. For it is not enough to know *what* we *ought* to say; we must also say it *as* we ought.' After a short reference to the importance of delivery, which is regarded as largely a natural gift, the first four chapters deal with *lexis*, in its more limited sense of *diction*, or the choice of words. In the diction of prose — and indeed in that of poetry also — clearness and fitness (propriety, appropriateness, decorum) are designated as the chief virtues. Faults of taste (*frigidities*, as the Greeks were fond of calling them) are discussed with examples; and after these, the right and wrong use of metaphor and simile. The next eight chapters deal more especially with words in combination, — with

[48]

composition in the sense of word-arrangement
(Greek, *synthesis;* Latin, *compositio*). Among
the topics treated are purity of idiom (c.5), am-
plitude of style (c.6), fitness (c.7), prose
rhythm (c.8), the period (c.9), vivacity (cc.
10,11), the chief differences between the literary (Greek, ' graphic,' i.e., ' written ') and the
controversial or debating style (c.12). The
remaining seven chapters (cc.13-19) are devoted to speech-structure (*taxis*). It is pointed
out that there are only two indispensable parts
in a speech: the statement of one's case, and
the arguments in its support. Exposition and
proof are the two essential things. But it is
usual to add a formal introduction and conclusion, and thus we have four divisions: (1)
proem, cc. 14,15; (2) statement of facts, c.16;
(3) arguments, cc. 17,18; (4) epilogue, c.19.
Aristotle neatly finishes the last chapter (book
III, c.19) of his entire work by taking a peroration, slightly adapted to suit his purpose, from
the *Eratosthenes* of the Attic orator Lysias.
After remarking that the disconnected style of
language is appropriate for a peroration, he
concludes as follows, though with a telling
brevity (there are four words altogether in the
Greek) which can hardly be kept in English:

' I have done. You have heard me. The facts are before you. I ask for your judgment.'

If we consider the work as a whole, the first book may perhaps be described as mainly logical and political, the second as mainly ethical or psychological, the third as mainly literary or stylistic. The speaker perhaps counts most in book I, the audience in book II, and the speech itself in book III. To the man who aspires to oratorical success, book I seems to say ' Be logical. Think clearly. Reason cogently. Remember that *argument* is the life and soul of persuasion'; book II, ' Study human nature. Observe the characters and emotions of your audience, as well as your own character and emotions '; book III, ' Attend to delivery. Use language rightly. Arrange your material well. End crisply.' And the whole treatise presupposes good wits and a fine general education. As to the art of Criticism, which has more scope in the third book than in the other two, we may recall that Dio Chrysostom (*Or.*53) says that Aristotle was regarded as its founder, and it is perhaps not fanciful to observe that if the *Rhetoric* begins with the Greek noun for ' rhetoric,' it ends with the Greek verb which inculcates ' judgment,' ' sift-

ing,' ' criticism.' *Judgment* prevails throughout it, and *literary* judgment is present where it
is called for. The same favourite word of
Aristotle's occurs in the *Politics* where we are
told that ' the many are better *judges* (*critics*)
than a single man of music and poetry; for
some understand one part, and some another,
and among them, they understand the whole.' [1]

For the sake of brevity, it will be well to pick
out a few leading topics from book III, and
then to pass on to Demetrius, whose work
stands in close connexion with book III, and
will, when compared with it in some detail,
leave a clear impression of the lasting influence
of Aristotle in rhetorical and literary study.
What, first, is Aristotle's definition of prose
style? It is given at the beginning of the second chapter in book III: ' Style (*lexis*) to be
good must be clear, as is proved by the fact that
speech which fails to convey a plain meaning
will fail to do just what speech has to do. It
must also be appropriate, avoiding both meanness and undue elevation; poetical language is
certainly free from meanness, but it is not appropriate to prose.' Aristotle seems here to be
adapting to the needs of prose (oratorical prose
especially) the shorter, but in the main ident-

[51]

ical, definition found in the *Poetics*, ' Style to be good must be clear and free from meanness.' [2] In prose he distrusts ornament, though he recognizes that a good prose style will rise and fall with its subject. Ornament, he feels, is apt to obscure the meaning and to lead to fine writing and flamboyant speaking; the diction of prose is, he declares, distinct from that of poetry. The key-notes of the definition in the *Rhetoric* are, therefore, *clearness* and *fitness*. The former is, with him and with all who followed his teaching, a primary essential. As he says above, in terms characteristic of his philosophy, ' speech which does not make the meaning plain will not perform its own proper work, or function.' As for ornament, it will be kept in its place by a sense of what is fitting — by a good taste which will shrink alike from excess and defect. It is conspicuously out of place in strict scientific investigation: ' nobody,' he says, ' uses fine language when teaching geometry,' [3] — a remark which the founders of our Royal Society would have approved emphatically.

It is towards the end of the first chapter in the same book that Aristotle distinguishes explicitly between poetic and prose diction. The

[52]

distinction thus drawn is of permanent value; and even in his day it had an historical aspect, as his careful statement, given on page 37 above, shows. After referring to the traditional difference between the language of prose and of poetry, he mentions the ' state of things to-day (i.e., in his own time), when even the language of tragedy has altered its character. Just as iambics were adopted (in tragedy), instead of (trochaic) tetrameters, because they are the most prose-like of all metres, so tragedy has given up all those words, not used in ordinary talk, which decorated the early drama and are still used by the writers of hexameter poems. It is therefore ridiculous to imitate a poetical manner which the poets themselves have dropped.' [4]

In the third chapter, examples are given of the bad taste shown by Gorgias and other rhetoricians when they misuse such poetical ornaments as compound words, which might find a fitting place in dithyrambs. Lycophron, we are told, talks of the ' *many-visaged* heaven ' above the ' *giant-crested* earth '; and Gorgias, of the ' *pauper-poet* flatterer.'

The twelfth chapter is of cardinal importance for any inquiry which includes literature as well

as oratory, literary criticism as well as rhetoric:
' Each kind of rhetoric has its own appropriate
style. The style of written prose is not that of
oratorical debate, nor are those of political and
forensic speaking the same. Both written and
spoken have to be known. To know the latter
is to know how to speak good Greek. To know
the former means that you are not obliged, as
otherwise you are, to hold your tongue when
you wish to communicate something to the general public.' [5] The whole of chapter 12 should
be read, and it will be seen that Aristotle carefully distinguishes the literary from the spoken
style. This express recognition, by him, of the
written word and its mission is noteworthy in
an age when the ear and the voice, rather than
the eye and the pen, conveyed the studied
thoughts of one man to another. Poems were,
in Greece, recited by rhapsodists or delivered
by actors; the histories of Herodotus and
Thucydides were read aloud by men trained to
the task; education in philosophy and science
was imparted by lecture or dialogue. Plato,[6]
in his paradoxical way, had thought little of
that art of writing which has preserved the entire body of his works for all future ages. Aristotle, with characteristic good sense, prizes an

art which enables a thinker to impart something to the world at large — that world beyond
the lecture-room which is contemplated in the
remarkable passage with which his logical
treatises end. From his special point of view in
the *Rhetoric*, he seems to group all ' literature '
under his third division of oratory, the epideictic. Political and forensic speeches, even
if written down beforehand, were intended for
delivery, rather than for reading. Epideictic
oratory, such as that of Isocrates, was coming
more and more to be a pamphlet, not a speech;
in theme and occasion it had never been so re-
stricted as the other branches of oratory. The
rhetorician Alcidamas, who was a contemporary of Isocrates and like him a pupil of Gorgias,
was as much devoted to practical oratory as
Isocrates to literary rhetoric, and composed a
diatribe, still extant,[7] in which extemporaneous
speech is extolled at the expense of written.
But Isocrates was right when he looked beyond
Athens and his own age, and thought that an
author should appeal to a wide public of intelligent readers. Alcidamas did not write to be
read, but through a Greek commentator's
written note on the *Rhetoric* Book I, c.13, we
still possess a memorable sentence from his

[55]

Messeniac Oration: ' God has left all men free; Nature has made no man a slave.'[8]

Aristotle observes that, while epideictic oratory is the most literary of all the branches of oratory, forensic oratory — particularly that addressed to a single judge — is more literary and finished than political. As he puts it, the oratory addressed to large parliamentary assemblies is 'like scene-painting'; or more strictly 'like drawing in light and shade,' without the use of colour. His remarks on the effect of dramatic delivery in producing liveliness and variety, and also in hiding weak literary workmanship, are so true that we feel he must often have listened with pleasure to good speakers and actors, and that in our day he would have liked to hear Eleonora Duse vary her tones as, in her beautiful Italian, she used to say ' *I* am *I.*'[9]

After thus broadly distinguishing the styles appropriate to the three great branches of oratory, Aristotle adds an observation which will carry us forward to Demetrius and later writers generally: ' To analyze style still further, and add that it must be *agreeable* or *magnificent,* is superfluous; for why should it have these traits any more than *restraint, liberality,* or any other

moral excellence? Obviously agreeableness
will be produced by the qualities already mentioned, if our definition of excellence of style
has been correct. For what other reason should
style be 'clear,' and not 'mean' but 'appropriate'? If it is prolix, it is not clear; nor yet
if it is curt. Plainly the middle way suits best.
Again, style will be made agreeable by the elements mentioned, namely by the good blending
of ordinary and unusual words, by the rhythm,
and by the persuasiveness that springs from
appropriateness.' [10]

The present writer has, in his recent edition [11]
of *Demetrius on Style,* put forward the view
that Demetrius belongs to the age of Plutarch.
However this may be, there can be no doubt
that he draws, directly or indirectly, from Peripatetic sources: particularly from the third
book of Aristotle's *Rhetoric* and from Theophrastus' lost work on *Style.* But in his division, which forms the framework of his book,
of literary expression, or style, into four types
(elevated, elegant, plain, and forcible), he is
clearly at variance with Aristotle who, in the
passage above quoted, deprecates any classification based on those many ethical traits which
might be taken to mark so personal a thing as

[57]

style.   Some of Aristotle's own friends and
pupils went further than he did, and he may
be criticizing one or other of them.   Quintilian [12] tells us that Theodectes wished the ex-
pository style to be not only ' magnificent ' but
' agreeable.'   Theophrastus,[13] too, seems to have
recognized ' magnificence ' and ' agreeableness '
as merits of style generally, but not perhaps to
have labelled any particular style as ' magnificent ' or ' agreeable.'   Any classification so
specific as ' Types of Style ' would seem to be
later than Theophrastus and may have originated in the desire, shared by the Peripatetic
and Stoic schools, to distinguish a strictly logical from a more ornamental or ' rhetorical ' way
of speaking and writing.[14]   But, once introduced, the classification had a great vogue
among the Greek and Latin writers on rhetorical subjects, and much that is best in ancient
literary criticism has come down to us in dis-
cussions of this kind.

In the first sentence of his essay, Demetrius
makes it clear that Prose Style, not Style in
general, is his immediate theme, though his
habit of drawing illustrations freely from the
poets extends in practice the range and value
of his work, the Greek title of which might be

[58]

paraphrased as 'Expression in Speech and Writing.' Demetrius opens with the unpretending but useful remark that, as verse owes its ordered movement to measures or metres, so is prose kept within due bounds by divisions of its own. The Greek names of these divisions survive to-day as terms of punctuation: 'comma,' 'colon,' and 'period' (full stop). The period, in the Greek sense of the word, engages Demetrius' special attention. He refers, with approval, to Aristotle's definition of it, 'By a period I mean a portion of speech which has in itself a beginning and an end, being at the same time not too big to be taken in at a glance'; [15] and he himself adds, pertinently, that the term implies a rounded structure and a thought held in suspense. When contrasting the free-running sentences of early writers such as Hecataeus and Herodotus with the periodic or rounded style which followed under the lead of Gorgias, he uses a noteworthy comparison: 'There is something trim and neat in the older method of writing. It resembles ancient statues, the art of which was thought to consist in their succinctness and spareness. The style of later writers is like the works of the sculptor Pheidias, since it already exhibits in some degree the union of grandeur with finish.'[16]   In invoking the analogy of another art, Demetrius tacitly recognizes that the principles of all fine art are the same.   In the next sentence, he puts forward as his own view one which is truly Peripatetic in its avoidance of extremes: 'My own personal view is that discourse should neither, like that of Gorgias, consist wholly of a string of periods, nor be wholly disconnected like the ancient writings, but should rather combine the two methods. It will then be elaborate and simple at the same time, and draw charm from both sources, being neither too untutored nor too artificial.'[17]   He condemns accumulated periods with endings which their sickened hearers foresee and forestall, and he would not have any period exceed the length of four clauses: a limitation which would have clipped the wings of Isocrates in a highly salutary way.   Three kinds of period are recognized and described by him: for narrative, dialogue, and oratory.   This division is not found in Aristotle; but, for the most part, Demetrius' introduction, in its treatment of the period and such related matters as rhythm and antithesis, agrees in essence with the third book of the *Rhetoric*.

In dealing with his main subject, the Four Types of Style, Demetrius offers no definition of Good Style in general. It is, as might be expected, in giving the characteristics of the plain style (that which distrusts ornament) that he comes nearest to Aristotle's definition. He pronounces lucidity to be the first essential of this style, and gives directions for its attainment, pointing out incidentally that brevity may hinder it. The other three styles make, he implies, in the pursuit of their special qualities, some sacrifice of the cardinal virtue of clearness. The elevated and the plain styles are, in his view, direct opposites. With this exception, the various styles may run into one another. ' In the poetry of Homer, for example, as well as in the prose of Plato, great elevation is joined to great force and charm.' [18] Demetrius stands alone, among extant writers (Peripatetic or non-Peripatetic), in introducing the ' forcible ' as a separate type of style. In initiating or adopting this classification, he seems to have been influenced by a desire to find a special place for Demosthenes, whom Dionysius, as we shall see later, regards as a master not of one style only but of all.

The Types of Style are non-Aristotelian.

But, in the treatise on *Style* as a whole, Peripatetic influence is pervasive. Everywhere the falsehood of extremes is before the writer's eye. Excessive imitation of the poets in prose is deprecated repeatedly.[19] One of the best things quoted from Aristotle's successor Theophrastus is this: 'Not all possible points should be punctiliously and tediously elaborated by a speaker, but some should be left to the comprehension and inference of the hearer who, when he perceives what you have left unsaid, becomes not only your hearer but your witness, and a very friendly witness too. For he thinks himself intelligent because you have afforded him the means of showing his intelligence. It seems like a slur on your hearer to tell him everything as though he were a simpleton.'[20] In other words, something should be left to the reader's own perception and imagination; it should be remembered that distinction of style is due not less to what is left unsaid than to what is said, and that 'le secret d'ennuyer est celui de tout dire.' It is good, too, to know how Theophrastus defined beautiful words: 'beauty in a word is that which appeals pleasantly to the ear or the eye, or has noble associations of its own.'[21]

A summary of the characteristics attributed by Demetrius to the Four Types of Style will be found elsewhere.[22] Here some special points may be picked at large from the various chapters, particularly points which show still further the Peripatetic affinities of the treatise. Demetrius begins as follows those excellent sections on the art of letter-writing which form part of his chapter on the Plain Style: ' We will next treat of the epistolary style, since it too should be plain. Artemon, the editor of Aristotle's *Letters,* says that a letter ought to be written in the same manner as a dialogue, a letter being regarded by him as one of the two sides of a dialogue. There is perhaps some truth in what he says, but not the whole truth. The letter should be a little more studied than the dialogue, since the latter counterfeits an extemporary utterance, while the former is committed to writing and is (in a manner) sent as a gift.'[23] Later he says, ' The letter, like the dialogue, should abound in glimpses of character. It may be said that everybody reveals his own soul in his letters. . . . A letter is designed to be the heart's good wishes in brief.'[24] How far Aristotle was the author of the *Letters* attributed to him in antiquity, we do not know.

Artemon, the editor here mentioned, lived some two centuries after Aristotle's death and another two centuries before the date we have ascribed to Demetrius. Together with Archedemus of Tarsus,[25] with whom he was probably contemporary, Artemon may thus be looked upon as a half-way house connecting Demetrius with the original Peripatetic School.

Metaphor and simile are treated by Demetrius under the Elevated Style. This is natural in a Peripatetic writer. Demetrius is Aristotelian when he says that well-chosen metaphors conduce to dignity of style, whereas familiar words, used not in a ' transferred ' sense but in their ' proper ' meaning, are apt to be held cheap.[26] He is also in agreement with *Rhetoric* Book III, c.4 and *Poetics* c.21 when (in the same passage) he says: " Metaphors should not be crowded together, or we shall find ourselves writing dithyrambic poetry in place of prose. Nor yet should they be far-fetched, but natural and based on a true analogy. There is a resemblance, for instance, between a general, a pilot, and a charioteer; for they are all in command. Accordingly it can safely be said that a general ' pilots ' the State, and conversely that a pilot ' commands ' the ship."

Then he adds, in humorous deprecation of Aristotle's excessive regard for the 'proportional' metaphor, "Not all metaphors can, however, be used convertibly like the above. Homer could call the lower slope of Mount Ida its 'foot,' but he could not go further and call a man's foot his 'slope'!" To Demetrius, as to Aristotle, the simile is an expanded metaphor, the expansion not being, in prose, so elaborate as to resemble poetical imagery.

In connexion with the elevated style, Demetrius touches on its besetting sin of 'frigidity,' that 'frost,' or chill, which the actors dread when their ardour fails to 'get across the footlights.' His treatment of the subject agrees with Aristotle's, but (as so often) goes beyond it, though without deserting Peripatetic principles. In one passage he names Theophrastus and may owe to him a surprising example which is not found in Aristotle: "We will first speak of the faulty style which is next neighbour to the elevated. Its name is 'frigid,' and 'the frigid' is defined by Theophrastus as that which exceeds the expression appropriate to the thought, for example

A cup unbased is not intabulated.

Here the meaning is: 'a cup without a bottom

is not placed upon a table.' The subject, being trivial, does not admit of such magniloquence." [27] This verse, so sharply and deservedly condemned, raises an interesting question of literary criticism. The offending line seems undoubtedly to come from a play of Sophocles, incredible as this may seem. The drama to which it is assigned is the *Triptolemus,* an early, but apparently a serious, play. What place can such a line have found in any tragedy? The present writer would suggest that it may possibly have been spoken by some drunken servitor, a homely sententious character resembling the watchman of the *Agamemnon;* and that it was lines thus introduced that Sophocles had mainly in mind when, as in the genial retrospect of his later years he described the gradual evolution of his literary style, he stated [28] that in his youth he had ' mocked the pomp of Aeschylus.'

Nothing is more satisfactory in Demetrius than his condemnation of bombast, bathos, preciosity and affectations of all sorts.[29] He sees that even so useful a device as antithesis can be overdone, and he has the courage to condemn such excess in a famous passage of Demosthenes' *Crown:* ' You were initiating, I was initiated; you taught, I attended classes; you took minor parts in the theatre, I was a spectator; you were driven off the boards, I hissed.' 'The elaborate parallelism of clauses,' comments Demetrius, 'produces the impression of false artifice; of trifling, rather than of honest indignation.' [30] In our own language, we can but regret Milton's close imitation (in the *Apology for Smectymnuus*) of this passage of Demosthenes, and we may perhaps also feel that even Burke's celebrated eulogy on John Howard suffers from a superabundance of contrasted clauses.

Under the Elegant, or Finished, Style Demetrius groups whatever is graceful or charming. He does not exclude jests and puns, provided they do not sin against good taste and breeding; as he says, there is some indication of a man's character in his jokes — in their playfulness or their license. His sections 163–172 should be compared with Aristotle's *Rhetoric* Book III, cc.11, 12, 18, and it should be noticed that he sometimes quotes from Aristophanes whom the Greek critics tend to ignore or censure.

Under the Forcible Style are illustrated, from Demosthenes, such devices as the rhetorical question ('Nay, Philip was appropriating

[67]

Euboea, and establishing a fortress to command Attica; and in so doing was he wronging us and violating the peace, or was he not? '), or the climax ('I did not speak thus, and then fail to move a resolution; I did not move a resolution, and then fail to act as an envoy; I did not act as an envoy, and then fail to convince the Thebans '). With regard to the latter excerpt from Demosthenes the critic says, truly, that " if it were rewritten thus, ' having expressed my views and moved a resolution, I acted as an envoy and convinced the Thebans,' it would be a mere recital of events, with nothing forcible about it." [31]

But it is in dealing with the Plain Style, the style which is sparing of ornament and oratorical device, that Demetrius, who himself writes plainly, is most helpful to the ordinary writer. He knows, and can make others know, that where there is deep and sincere feeling elaborate language is not needed, and that any touch of poetry or metaphor will move the hearer all the more in a simple setting. This simple vividness he attributes to the historian Ctesias in his description of the way in which news of the death of the younger Cyrus at the battle of Cunaxa came to his mother Parysatis.[32] The metaphor (' In the bivouac of the brave ') here put into the Greek messenger's mouth, by Ctesias, who was a doctor as well as a historian and had a doctor's kindliness and tact, is no other than that with which Theodore O'Hara concludes his well-known lines. The best of the Greek literary critics all show this appreciation of truth, sincerity, simplicity, naturalness. Plato sees in truth the foundation of all good writing.[33] Demetrius praises unadorned simplicity,[34] and might well have quoted the line of Aeschylus, ' Simple, aye simple are the words of truth.' [35] If there must be art (as there surely must) it must be hidden, as Aristotle prescribes: ' A writer must disguise his art and give the impression of speaking naturally and not artificially. Naturalness is persuasive, artificiality is the contrary; for our hearers are prejudiced and think we have some design against them, as if we were mixing their wines for them.' [36]

It should be noticed that Demetrius never uses the word 'rhetoric,' and that when he refers to ' rhetoricians ' there is sometimes a shade of irony or contempt, as with us to-day. We must think of him as composing, long after Aristotle's time, an essay which is deeply indebted to the third book of the *Rhetoric,* but is itself a general art of prose composition, meant for speakers and writers alike, and contains by the way much valuable literary criticism. His standards are high because they rest on the study and appreciation not of late authors but of the classics of Greece, ' the ancients ' as he calls them; and not only of prose-authors like Plato and Thucydides, but of poets like Homer and Sappho. The York Demetrius (who is probably identical with Plutarch's Demetrius of Tarsus) dedicated one of his two votive tablets ' to Oceanus and Tethys,' and may thus have been recalling, now that his lot was cast among ' ultimos orbis Britannos,' the lines in which Hera addresses Zeus, ' I go to visit the utmost bounds of the fruitful earth, and Oceanus, father of the gods, and mother Tethys.' [37] It is pleasant to indulge the fancy, if it be no more than fancy, that the York Demetrius wrote the essay on *Style,* and that our author was thus, under the wing of Agricola, the precursor of classical education for Britain and for a New York which then existed in dreams only.

IV. DIONYSIUS OF HALICARNASSUS

THE date of Demetrius is a matter of conjecture. Dionysius we know, on his own testimony, to have been living in Rome (that 'most frequented and most hospitable of cities') from 30 B.C. to 8 B.C.; he was probably still living there at the time of Christ's birth. During the twenty-two years he has specified, he was busily employed as a teacher of Greek literature and of Greek views on public speaking, to Roman youths of good family, and as a writer both on these topics and on the early history of Rome. For his historical work, which is of little moment, he learned Latin in order to consult Roman authorities whom he names. In his Greek literary essays, which are thorough and wide-ranging, he refers to no Latin writer or speaker: not even to Cicero, who died but 13 years before he came to Rome, nor to Horace, who died in 8 B.C., when he was still residing there. But, in the Preface to his *Ancient Orators,* he acknowledges gratefully the debt due to those public men of Rome who,

[71]

in his own and earlier days, had encouraged the
Greek literary world to revert to the best Attic
models of speaking and writing, and to repudi-
ate those pestilent affectations which, after the
death of Alexander, had for many generations
flaunted themselves in the ' dens of Asia.' In
his work for this Attic revival during the age of
Augustus, he had, as a Greek coadjutor, the
critic Caecilius of Calacte, whose name is
coupled with his own in two of the three passages in which Quintilian mentions Dionysius.[1]

On the side of oratory, it was the more obviously practical rhetoric of Isocrates that Dionysius wished to encourage at Rome, rather
than the rhetoric of the philosophers. A curious
literary letter survives to show his attitude.
Some Peripatetic philosopher of that day, look-
ing back three hundred years, had undertaken
to prove that the *Rhetoric* of Aristotle was
earlier than the speeches of Demosthenes, who
owed his success as an orator to the observance
of its precepts. Dionysius, in a Letter addressed to his friend Ammaeus, denies this
reckless assertion, and seeks to show that
Demosthenes was at the height of his fame, and
had delivered his most celebrated speeches (including that on the *Crown*, 330 B.C.), at the

time when Aristotle wrote his *Rhetoric*. His
main contention is fully proved, despite occasional over-statements; and the Letter itself is
still a leading authority for the chronology of
the lives and activities of both Demosthenes
and Aristotle.[2] In it Dionysius has shown that
he possesses at least one important qualifica-
tion of a literary historian: he knows how to
compare dates. As he says elsewhere: ' in such
investigations the discrimination of dates is indispensable.'[3] He also makes his own many-
sided obligations clear when he says that he
would not have it thought, by students of public
oratory, that ' all the precepts of rhetoric are
included in the Peripatetic philosophy, and that
nothing important has been discovered by men
such as Theodorus, Thrasymachus and Antiphon, nor by Isocrates, Anaximenes and Alcidamas, nor by their contemporaries who composed rhetorical handbooks and engaged in
oratorical contests — such men as Theodectes,
Philiscus, Isaeus and Cephisodorus, together
with Hypereides, Lycurgus, and Aeschines.'[4]
There is no doubt that, in his literary essays
generally, Dionysius cast his net wide and far
back. For us this is one of his chief merits; he
preserves the spirit of much lost criticism that

[73]

is almost as old as Greek artistic prose itself;
and though he is not inclined to over-value the
philosophers, there are not wanting many passages which show or confess indebtedness to
Aristotle and Theophrastus, alike for details
and for principles.[5]

To Isocrates, as the creator of a standard
type of literary rhetorical prose, Dionysius de-
votes one of those excellent essays on the Attic
Orators which, with their biographical details
and their searching examination (well sup-
ported by ample quotations) of formal characteristics in their historical development, consti-
tute, within their limits, as near an approach to
a History of Literature as Greek antiquity has
transmitted to us. In this essay and elsewhere,
he praises Isocrates as man and writer, but in
no uncritical way. He sees his great importance in the evolution of Greek prose style, and
discerns in him a certain nobility of aim. ' The
strongest exhortations to virtue are to be found
in the speeches of Isocrates. I maintain that
those who would learn the secret of political
power, not in part only but in its fullness,
should have this orator at their fingers' ends.
. . . He proclaims (in one of his speeches)
that it is not a fleet of warships, nor Greeks

governed by force, that make Athens great, but
righteous aims and the succour of the wronged.'
At the same time Dionysius is quite alive to
such weak points in Isocrates as his excessive
regard for smoothness of style and a pleasant
cadence. 'The thought is often the slave of
rhythmical expression, and truth is sacrificed to
elegance. . . . Now the natural course is for
the expression to follow the ideas, not the ideas
the expression.' His tameness and verbosity
are condemned thus: 'He cannot move his
hearers as far as he desires, and for the most
part he does not even desire it. . . . His style
[in a certain passage] should have struck home
like a blow. As a matter of fact, it is supple and
smooth, and glides noiselessly through the ear
like oil.' To how many writers and speakers
since Dionysius' day might this excellent piece
of literary criticism — this lifelike sketch of
good points and bad — be applied!

Other Attic Orators to whom Dionysius de-
votes separate essays are Lysias, Isaeus, and
Demosthenes. Lysias is praised for such qualities as his purity of expression, his gift of characterization and his unfailing sense of fitness,
his vividness and his inimitable charm. His
simplicity and directness are admirably illus-

trated by means of a few narrative sentences taken by Dionysius from a speech now lost.[6] It is said of him that, ' though he seems to talk like ordinary people, there is a world of difference between him and ordinary people.' In reference to Isaeus he remarks, ' If I were asked why I have included Isaeus, imitator as he is of Lysias, I should give as my reason that in his speeches are to be sought, as it seems to me, the germs and first-beginnings of the oratorical power of Demosthenes, which is universally regarded as the height of perfection.' Highly as Isaeus is for this reason esteemed by Dionysius, he is in at least one important respect rated lower than Lysias. His speeches do not seem so natural as those of his predecessor. ' Anyone reading the narrative passages of Lysias, far from suspecting art or trickery, would rather discern the promptings of nature and truth, overlooking the simple fact that the imitation of nature is the highest triumph of art.'[7]

Dionysius refers to the oratorical supremacy of Demosthenes as a universally admitted fact: we know to-day, perhaps more fully than he did, how greatly this recognition was furthered by the sound judgment of Cicero and other distinguished Romans, who, like Hamlet's ' sta-

tists,' held it 'a baseness to write fine' in the
Asiatic manner, — the manner of those mixed
populations in Asia whose use of the Greek language was not controlled by the best Greek
taste of an earlier age. He also emphasizes his
own view that, among the orations of Demosthenes, the *Crown* holds the foremost place.
Something of the same kind might, truly
enough, be said of Dionysius' own essay on
Demosthenes. In its own way, and within its
own bounds, it deserves the title of 'master-
piece' which has been given to it. Into none of
his studies of the Greek orators has Dionysius
thrown himself with more vigour and enthusiasm. It is his delight to show that Demosthenes
'disdained to be an imitator of any single style
or man. He saw that all alike were half-
finished and incomplete, and from them all he
chose and wove together the best and most useful elements, and fashioned one language out
of many. . . . His style resembles the fabled
Proteus of our ancient poets.' Moreover, the
effect of his speeches on their readers is wonderful, and the effect on their original hearers
must have been more wonderful still: 'When
I take up one of his speeches I am entranced
and carried hither and thither, stirred now by

this emotion, now by that. I feel distrust, anxiety, fear, contempt, hatred, pity, good-will, anger, jealousy. I am agitated by every passion in turn that can sway the human heart, and feel in no way different from those who are being initiated into wild mystic rites. . . . When we who are parted by centuries from the time of Demosthenes, and are in no way affected by the matters at issue, are thus moved and overcome and borne wherever the argument leads us, how must the Athenians of that day and the Greeks generally have been carried away, when living interests of their own were at stake, and when the great orator, whose reputation stood so high, spoke from the heart, and laid bare the inmost feelings that inspired his soul? '

From Demosthenes to Deinarchus is a long step downwards. Deinarchus was the last and least important of the ' Ten Attic Orators '; he was sometimes called ' the barley Demosthenes,' being as much coarser than Demosthenes as barley is than fine wheat, or (possibly) as beer is when compared with wine; he was, in fact, like the poet Crabbe, a ' Pope in worsted stockings.' Minor author though he may be, Dionysius treats him in a way which well illustrates the scrupulous thoroughness and

independence of the critic's studies.[8] A good
example of his application of chronological
tests occurs where he rejects a certain speech
of Deinarchus by determining its date on de-
cisive internal evidence and then drily remarking that ' Deinarchus at that time had not yet
reached his tenth year.' It may be added here
that Dionysius is said to have defined rhetoric
as ' the artistic faculty of persuasive argument
on a matter of public interest: its end being
good speaking.' [9]

Oratory is the preoccupation of Dionysius in
his essays, but (as with the Greek critics generally) not to the exclusion of other branches of
composition, prose and verse. As an historian,
he is interested in historians, especially in their
relation to speech-writing; and being himself
a native of Halicarnassus, he has a special interest in Herodotus, who was born at Halicarnassus some four centuries before him. In his
essay on Thucydides (no separate writing of
his on Herodotus has come down to us, though
the scattered references to him are numerous),
he praises, rightly, the epic charm with which
Herodotus tells his story. Elsewhere he commends his choice, and treatment, of subject, and
contrasts him in this respect with Thucydides.

[79]

Though he often seems not to appreciate the philosophic depth of the great Athenian historian and is apt to confound history with panegyric, it is pleasant to find him not so entirely an ' Atticist ' as to forget, as modern students of Greek have often done, that the Ionian Greek of Herodotus, and of Homer, suggests more vividly a world beyond Athens, and beyond Greece itself, than the strict Attic could ever do.

For the style of Thucydides, Dionysius has both praise and blame. He can transcribe a really great passage, the narrative of the Athenian naval disaster in the Great Harbour of Syracuse, and pay a really fine tribute to it. On the other side, he criticizes, bit by bit, the elaborate language in which Thucydides describes the havoc wrought in the minds of men by the spread of a revolutionary spirit throughout the cities of Greece.[10] The general conclusion reached is that the narrative pages are, with few exceptions, altogether admirable and adapted for every kind of use, whereas the passages that resemble harangues are not, in every case, suitable for imitation. The word ' imitation ' gives the key to Dionysius' strictures. We have always to remember that imitation of standard authors was a regular part of the

training given in the rhetorical schools of
Greece and Rome, and that Thucydides, and
Plato, were among the writers thus prescribed.
We can easily imagine the absurdities to which
the attempts of ambitious young orators to ape
Thucydides must have led. Like imitators
generally, they would no doubt catch the mannerisms rather than the manner, the eccentrici-
ties rather than the true excellences, of the
great original. As Cicero caustically puts it,
' once they have uttered a few broken and gap-
ing phrases, each of them thinks himself a regular Thucydides.' [11]

' You can almost count on your fingers,' says
Dionysius, ' the people who are capable of com-
prehending the whole of Thucydides; and not
even they can do so without occasional recourse
to a grammatical commentary.' Such obscurity he condemns as ' ruining all fine things and
shrouding merits in darkness.' [12] This fault in
Thucydides he traces to what is one of its chief
causes, the desire for brevity; and this desire
is part of the struggle of genius to express itself
forcibly in the imperfect medium of language.
Dionysius has often, and with reason, been ac-
cused of showing pedantry in some of his critical conclusions. But, on points of Greek style,

his perceptions are more acute than ours, and he is on sure ground when he classes Thucydides and the orator Antiphon together as representatives of the ' austere ' composition. A modern editor of Thucydides has suggested as typical of his manner a sentence, describing the calamities inflicted on Hellas by the Peloponnesian War, which Jowett translates thus: ' Never were so many cities captured and de-populated — some by Barbarians, others by Hellenes themselves fighting against one another; and several of them after their capture were repeopled by strangers. Never were exile and slaughter more frequent, whether in the war or brought about by civil strife.' If the original sentence be examined carefully in the the Greek,[18] it will be found to contain many of the ' colours ' of style which Dionysius [14] sees in Thucydides: such as pregnant brevity, a rugged austerity of movement (not for Thucydides the smooth glide of Isocrates, with no vowel meeting vowel), gravity, vehemence, and the power of stirring the emotions. It should be added that Dionysius censures the poetical element in Thucydides' vocabulary, a point in which Thucydides follows Gorgias but was not followed by Isocrates or Aristotle, both of

whom distinguish between the diction of prose
and poetry. Thucydides agrees with Gorgias
too, as Dionysius sees, in sometimes balancing
clause against clause in sound as well as in
antithetic sense, and in often preferring to the
free-running style that elaborate structure of a
sentence in which a conclusion kept in view
throughout is reached, after much suspense,
through the artistic unity of the ' period.'

The author — Cornificius presumably — of
the earliest extant Roman treatise on the art of
public speaking names three requisites for oratorical excellence: *ars, imitatio, exercitatio,* or
(1) the theory of rhetoric, (2) imitation, (3)
practice. It is a fear of the harm which might
be done to his own Roman pupils by a blind and
foolish ' imitation ' of so great a genius as
Plato that has caused Dionysius to be sus-
pected, by modern readers, of great folly and
narrowness himself. But his special point of
view, on which he often insists, must always be
borne in mind: no practical teacher of English
composition would, without many misgivings,
see his average pupils engaged in the ' imitation ' of Carlyle or Ruskin. In regard to ' composition,' in the limited sense of *the musical
arrangement of words,* Dionysius can impute

no blame to Plato. On the contrary he writes that Plato " has a perfect genius for discovering good melody and good rhythm, and if he had only been as able in the choice of words as he is unrivalled in the art of combining them, he ' had even outstript ' Demosthenes, so far as beauty of style is concerned, or ' had left the issue in doubt.' As it is, he is sometimes quite at fault in his choice of words; most of all when he is aiming at a lofty, unusual, elaborate style of expression." [15]

In not one but many of his essays, Dionysius attacks Plato's vocabulary as poetic and high-flown. He denounces it as sometimes ' dithy-rambic,' taking the word out of Plato's own mouth, in a burst of triumph which ignores the fact that Plato is a master of irony everywhere and not least in those two writings — the *Phaedrus* and the *Menexenus* — in which Dionysius seeks for ' speeches' without seeing that Plato's ' speeches ' are often strongly spiced with parody. It is true that Plato's diction borrows largely from the poets he banishes, and we are glad to see the point brought out by a Greek student of Greek who, though he lived long after Aristotle, shares Aristotle's healthy dislike for the excesses of Gorgias. It is interesting, too, in a disputed matter of literary history, to note that Dionysius is at one with Aristotle [16] in seeing in the ' Funeral Oration,' as both Aristotle and he call the *Menexenus,* a genuine work of Plato. But, for his own credit, we could wish that he had not, with the teacher's narrowness, been so intent upon driving home a particular lesson as to seem now and then to forget that Plato is, after all, one of the world's greatest philosophers and most consummate artists.

Still, Dionysius' essay on the (euphonic) *Arrangement of Words (De Compositione Verborum),* in which, as seen above, Plato is praised for his composition of words and blamed for their selection, is in its own way an excellent and illuminating piece of work. The average Englishman or American is apt to scoff at a modern French literary critic like Jules Lemaître when, being more directly in the Greek and Roman tradition, he frankly recognizes ' des finesses qui ne tiennent qu'à l'arrangement des mots.' But when an earlier Frenchman, a student of the Greek Dionysius, extols a well-known French author who ' D'un mot mis en sa place enseigna le pouvoir,' [17] let the Englishman or American no longer mock at this enthu-

siasm but think of some great line in his own
great language, such as Marlowe's:

*Cut is the branch that might have grown full
straight.*

We can imagine Dionysius saying that, even
though every single word in this line should be
scrupulously retained, yet the line itself would
be ruined if the order of just two words were
to be changed:

*The branch is cut that might have grown full
straight.*

Would he be wrong? Was not the poet-critic
Coleridge right in offering, as a rough definition of poetry, 'the best words in the best
order'? Was he not right in asking whether,
in Wordsworth's lines 'In distant countries I
have been,' a rustic, though he might well have
used the same words, would have placed them
in the same *order?*

Dionysius' treatment of his strict subject,
verbal arrangement, is in practice so wide-
ranging that it is convenient to describe his
work as an essay on Literary Composition
generally. The special problem of the harmonious arrangement of beautiful words is discussed in connexion with the whole art and
craft of literature. The essays on the Attic

Orators are concerned with prose and are accompanied by prose illustrations. The treatise
on Composition draws freely from the poets,
Homer especially. Homer, whom so many
modern scholars have thought to be artless, is
assumed by Dionysius to have spared no pains
over the art he loves; [18] consummate poets in
all ages are, Dionysius feels, also consummate
craftsmen. In the belief, shared by all the best
Greek literary critics, that a student of prose-
writing had lessons to learn from the Greek
poets as well as from Demosthenes or Plato,
Dionysius quotes the *Aphrodite* of Sappho, the
Danaë of Simonides, and a dithyramb of Pindar, and has thus preserved for posterity fragments of great poetry which but for him would
have been entirely lost. And if on the literary
side his good judgment is shown in the choice
anthology which his quotations form, or again
in such stray phrases as those which describe
Homer as ' of all poets the most many-voiced '
and attribute to Thucydides ' an old-world and
masterful nobility of style,' [19] there is also in his
general handling of his theme much of that
scientific thoroughness which the Greeks pur-
sued. He plans his inquiry in a systematic
way; and seeking to penetrate the secrets of

beautiful speech, he throws much incidental light on matters to us so difficult and obscure as Greek music, Greek accent, Greek phonetics and pronunciation. The book which results is unique: no other of its kind has come down to us from classical antiquity. If we desire to appreciate, so far as a modern student can, the formal side of that Greek literature in which form and substance are so closely knit together, we shall neglect the *De Compositione* at our peril. Epicurus is reported in it to have said that writing ' involves no labour.' [20] Dionysius expresses the worthier and more usual Greek view when, at the end of an eloquent outburst, he exclaims: ' It appears to me far more reasonable for a man who is composing public speeches, enduring memorials of his own powers, to attend even to the slightest details, than it is for the disciples of painters and of workers in relief, who display the dexterity and industry of their hands in a perishable medium, to expend the finished resources of their art on veins and down and bloom and other trifles of the kind.' [21]

The Greek sensitiveness to good melody and rhythm is vividly described in another passage: " Who is there that is not enthralled by the spell

of one melody while he remains unaffected in
any such way by another, that is not captivated
by this rhythm while that does but jar upon
him? Ere now I myself, even in the most popular theatres, thronged by a mixed and uncul-
tured multitude, have seemed to observe that
all of us have a sort of natural appreciation for
correct melody and good rhythm. I have seen
an accomplished harpist, of high repute, hissed
by the public because he struck a single false
note and so spoilt the melody. I have seen,
too, a flute-player, who handled his instrument
with the practised skill of a master, suffer the
same fate because he blew thickly or, through
not compressing his lips, produced a harsh
sound or so-called ' broken note ' as he played.
Nevertheless, if the amateur critic were sum-
moned to take up the instrument and himself
to render any of the pieces with whose perform-
ance by professionals he was just now finding
fault, he would be unable to do it. Why so?
Because this is an affair of technical skill, in
which we are not all partakers; the other of
feeling, which is nature's universal gift to man.
I have noticed the same thing occur in the case
of rhythms. Everybody is vexed and annoyed
when a performer strikes an instrument, takes

a step, or sings a note, out of time, and so destroys the rhythm." [22]

By his detailed analysis and his careful phonetic explanations Dionysius is able to make even a modern reader realize that the beauty of a Greek verse or of a Greek prose sentence largely depends upon the harmonious collocation of those *sounds* of which human speech primarily consists and that, in the best writers, the sound is echo to the sense. In his eleventh chapter he says expressly that ' the science of public oratory is a sort of musical science, differing from vocal and instrumental music in degree, not in kind,' and we owe largely to him any understanding we may have of the music of the Greek language. The measure of his success in proving his special point can be gauged only by reference to the original Greek of his illustrations and contentions. Here it will be enough to say that he distinguishes three *harmonies* in verbal composition: the austere, the smooth, and the intermediate. With regard to rhythm in particular he is in general agreement with Aristotle who says that ' The form of a prose composition should be neither metrical nor destitute of rhythm. The metrical form destroys the hearer's trust by its artificial ap-

pearance, and at the same time it diverts his
attention, making him watch for metrical re-
currences. . . . On the other hand, unrhyth-
mical language is too unlimited; we do not want
the limitations of metre, but some limitation we
must have, or the effect will be vague and un-
satisfactory. Now it is number that limits all
things; and it is the numerical limitation of the
form of a composition that constitutes rhythm,
of which metres are definite sections. Prose,
then, is to be rhythmical, but not metrical, or it
will become not prose but verse. It should not
even have too precise a prose rhythm, and
therefore should only be rhythmical to a certain
extent.' [23]

Although Dionysius refers, in support of his
views on prose rhythm, to the authority of
Aristotle ' in the third book of the Rhetorical
Arts,' [24] we cannot help feeling that he is more
ready than Aristotle would have been to detect
and welcome actual lines of verse in standard
prose. Though writing on oratory, Aristotle
has the scientific man's love for the precise
statement of thought; and this is endangered if
rhythm, by approaching the regularity of law,
passes into metre. The paeon, which Aristotle
favours at the beginning and end of sentences,

might little impede exact expression, for it has
not the marked metrical character which belongs to the iambus and the trochee, or to the
dactyl and the anapaest. Dionysius' real master in this matter may be conjectured to be Isocrates who is said to have laid it down that
'prose must not be merely prose, or it will be
dry; nor metrical, or its art will be undis-
guised; but it should be compounded with any
sort of rhythm, particularly iambic or trochaic.' [25] Similarly Dionysius would like to see
'metres and rhythms unobtrusively introduced
into prose.' [26] Cicero, who in agreement with
Aristotle's conception of 'rhythm' translates
the Greek word by 'numeros,' regards a metrical line in prose as a deformity; and (in agreement here with Theophrastus) he holds that
prose should be rhythmical not in any rigid way
but with some laxity.[27] As to modern English
prose-writers, the metres into which they drop
are usually of the iambic or trochaic order.
This is so with Ruskin and Carlyle, with Dick-
ens and Blackmore. But, as in ancient so in
modern times, the best criticism looks with
favour on rhythmical, with disfavour on metrical prose. Prose, it is held, loses its true character — as the minister primarily of reason

rather than of emotion and music — if it is made to conform to the strict laws of metre.

Dionysius himself applies the true corrective to any undue rigidity when he proclaims the supremacy of *variety*,[28] in regard to rhythm and the other elements of style. Variety is the natural corollary of *propriety* (or *fitness*), the adaptation of our speech to the complex requirements of character, feeling, occasion, subject-matter, and the like. But even variety, we are told, must not be carried to excess; uniformity is sometimes just as pleasing; tact is needed, and to impart tact is no easy task. 'We must keep in view good taste (more literally, *the right season*), for this is the best criterion of charm and its opposite. But about good taste no rhetorician or philosopher has, so far, produced a definite treatise. The man who first undertook to write on the subject, Gorgias of Leontini, achieved nothing worthy of mention. The nature of the subject, indeed, is not such that it can fall under any comprehensive and systematic treatment, nor can good taste in general be apprehended by science, but only by personal judgment. Those who have continually trained this latter faculty in many connexions are more successful than others in attaining good taste, while those who leave it untrained are rarely successful, and only by a sort of lucky stroke.' [29] The author who wrote these frank and discriminating words can have been no ' rhetorician ' in any invidious sense: he believes that training can do much but that in, say, the matter of euphony, the last appeal must be to ' the instinctive perception of the ear.' [30] He is clearly alive to the presence in style of much that eludes analysis and definition.

To sum up: the special merit of Dionysius is to have carried his pupils and readers back to the great epochs of Greece, but with an independent judgment which makes him ready to condemn even a famous writer when sinning against the fundamental laws of clearness and simplicity. He maintains, for example, that the style of Thucydides was exceptional even in his own day, and he combats the view that an historian (as distinguished, say, from an advocate) may plead in excuse for an artificial manner that he does not write for ' people in the market-place, in workshops or in factories, nor for others who have not shared in a liberal education, but for men who have reached rhetoric and philosophy after passing through a full curriculum of systematic studies, to whom therefore none of these expressions will appear unfamiliar.'[31] Obscurity and eccentricity, he says in effect, are not virtues except in the eyes of literary coteries; presumably a speaker speaks, and a writer writes, in order to be understood. In the *Literary Composition,* Homer is to Dionysius the great exemplar of simplicity. In his third chapter are quoted the first sixteen lines of the Sixteenth *Odyssey:* the homely scene in which Telemachus, returning from his visit to the Peloponnese, comes to the swineherd's hut, where Odysseus the world-wanderer is. The critic's comments are: " Everybody would, I am sure, testify that these lines cast a spell of enchantment on the ear, and rank second to no poetry whatsoever, however exquisite it may be. But what is the secret of their fascination, and what causes them to be what they are? Is it the selection of words, or the composition? No one will say ' the selection ': of that I am convinced. For the diction consists, warp and woof, of the most ordinary, the humblest words, such as might have been used off-hand by a farmer, a seaman, an artisan, or anybody else who takes no account of elegant speech."[32]

In his eagerness to magnify the ' composition ' of the Homeric passage, Dionysius per-

haps depreciates unduly its 'diction'; not
many, if any, of the words used would appear
to be 'cheap' or 'mean,' as his two epithets
strictly signify; taken as a whole, they are simple enough but with the simplicity of art.
Homer is an artist who knows that 'ars est
celare artem.' And many of the simplest
Homeric expressions bespeak a refined society.
Nausicaa's 'Pappa dear' [33] does not belong to a
rude age in the history of mankind; nor in such
an age would Charis be represented as having
one single word at her call when, in welcoming
Thetis, she reminds her that she is no *frequent-
visitor*.[34]

With the noble rhythms of Homer Dionysius
contrasts, rather cruelly, those of Hegesias, the
third-century rhetorician. Hegesias typifies to
him the decline in Greek literature which followed the death of Alexander, whose exploits
he, as the leader of the degenerate 'Asiatic'
school, had recorded with a feeble magniloquence. Hegesias' jerky style, with its eccen-
tric word-order, is an abomination to Dionysius, as may be seen from various references
and quotations throughout the *Literary Composition*. After giving an amusing parody of
Hegesias, Cicero remarks: 'Here you have the

style of Hegesias, *which Varro praises.*' [35] How
often, unhappily, have men of learning, both in
America and England, been found to praise
ambitious prose-writers for a vicious straining
after effect which has played strange pranks
with the natural order of words. Dionysius, on
the other hand, in his entire attitude not only
towards Homer but towards Sappho and Simonides, Herodotus and Demosthenes, has proved
that he can rise above the debased standards
of the ages immediately preceding his own, and
can discern and proclaim a classic excellence.
He has thus contributed not a little to confirm
our belief in the essential continuity of critical
principles — in the existence of a firm and permanent basis for the judgments of taste.[36]

V. OTHER CRITICS AND RHETORICIANS

IN starting a chapter which finds us in the midst of the Graeco-Roman world before and after the birth of Christ, it is well to ask what equivalents the Greeks had for that elaborate and comprehensive Latin-derived word 'literature' which we now find indispensable. Sometimes the term λόγοι, *logoi* ('speeches,' 'discourses') served the turn. Though often used specially of oratory or of prose, it had in practice a wider range, because of the oral character of all early literature.[1] Thus our natural modern equivalent for φιλόλογοι, *philologoi,* in a passage of Aristotle's *Rhetoric,* is *literary:* 'though they (the Lacedaemonians) are the least *literary* of men.'[2] The beautiful Greek word for 'music' sometimes includes literature, as one of those refined and harmonious arts over which the Muses preside. But the nearest etymological ancestor to 'literature,' and the one which marks most clearly the transition from speech to writing, is γράμματα, *grammata,* 'letters,' or (from the same root) γραφαί, graphai, 'writings.' In Plato's *Apology*, 'ignorant of letters' seems to mean 'ignorant of literature.'[3] In the *Rhetoric*, 'the graphic (written) style' means 'the literary style' or 'literature' in general.[4] In Quintilian's time, *litteratura* was used to translate the Greek γραμματική, grammaticē;[5] and from this source comes our word 'literature.' *Grammaticē* included the study of literature, particularly of poetry; and the corresponding term, γραμματικός, grammatikos (Lat., *grammaticus*), consequently meant a man of letters; a student, or a teacher, of literature. Side by side with *grammaticus* there existed, among Greeks and Romans, the name *criticus*, which still more definitely designated the literary *critic*. Dionysius, for example, was known in antiquity no less than to-day as a *critic*.

The direct descendants of Aristotle in the art of criticism (broadly understood as the sifting, or discrimination, of literature) were the scholars of Alexandria; and these, bettering here the example of Aristotle, were specially concerned to preserve the correct text of Homer, the greatest service of all. Aristarchus, who may well be reckoned the founder of scientific scholarship, seems to have acted upon the excellent literary and historical principle that each author is his own best interpreter. It is, however, not possible to say much about the contributions of Alexandrian scholars to literary criticism in general, since their writings have mostly perished, or survive only in annotations concerned chiefly with textual or verbal criticism. Still, the constant exercise of literary discrimination is implied in the classified lists of standard writers which they, or contemporary scholars elsewhere, are said to have issued; Alexandria giving attention to the poets (though the scholar-poet Callimachus included prose-writers in his comprehensive catalogue of literary celebrities), while Pergamum (and afterwards Caecilius, the friend of Dionysius) seems to have framed similar canons of the Attic Orators. The preservation of the extant *scholia,* or Greek annotations on Greek authors, we owe largely to the prodigious industry of the scholar Didymus, who, himself a contemporary of Dionysius, made full use of the commentaries of Aristarchus, who lived a century earlier, and of other Alexandrians earlier still.[6] It is needless to give any surviving specimens of the literary (as distinguished from textual or verbal) criti-

cism in which the lesser men of Alexandria were
prone to censure Homer and in so doing displayed their own prosy pedantry and triviality.
Zenodotus, in particular, seems to have shown
an inept and captious blindness to the simplicity of the heroic age. Evidence of a broader
view has been noted already in Aristarchus and
will be seen presently in Eratosthenes.

Some literary interest attaches to remarks
occasionally found in the *scholia* on the dramatic poetry of Greece, as to details of the
actor's art. We have a scholiast saying, in
reference to a Greek word which comes outside
the metre, after line 222 of the *Birds* of Aristophanes, ' This is a stage-direction, showing
that a musician is imitating [on the flute, or
clarinet] the nightingale which is still within the
copse.' On Sophocles' *Electra* 830, we are told
that the actor who played the part of Electra
should, at this point, raise his hands towards
heaven as if in accusation of the gods. On
Euripides' *Orestes* 279, we hear of an actor's
slip in enunciation which, with comic effect (cp.
Aristophanes, *Frogs*, 304), transformed ' calm
weather ' into a ' weasel '; and again, on line
1366, of an actor's long and dangerous leap.
This traditional Greek interest in the actor's

art is reflected in more than one passage of
Demetrius: for example, in that in which he
describes the 'many opportunities of movement offered to the actor by Ion's rush [when
Ion, in Euripides' play of that name, threatens
the swan] for his bow and arrows, by his face
upturned to the sky as he talks to the swan,
and by the rest of the detail contrived to aid
the actor.'[7]

The character of the *scholia* on prose-writers
may be illustrated by one or two not unfavourable examples. On the *Phaedrus* 261A, there is
one which is of interest to the student of rhetoric. Socrates wishes to persuade Phaedrus
that, unless he becomes a competent philosopher, neither will he ever become a competent
speaker on any subject. The scholiast comments, 'for the best speakers have also been
philosophers, just as Pericles was a disciple of
Anaxagoras and Demosthenes of Plato.' The
last statement might have angered Dionysius,
but Plutarch quotes fairly early authority for
it.[8] In any case, it cannot be ruled out by
Dionysius' chronological tests, since Demosthenes would be between thirty and forty when
Plato's long life ended. Thucydides, on the
other hand, died some twenty years before De-

mosthenes' birth, and so can have influenced
the orator, whose style seems to have been
deeply indebted to him, by his History only,
and not by any personal contact. Two Thucyd-
idean *scholia* are as follows: (1) where
Thucydides (Book I, c.22) describes his work
as ' a possession for ever rather than the exploit
of an hour,' the commentator remarks that in
this contrast Thucydides is hinting at the seductive narrative and fabulous stories of Herodotus
(fitted, no doubt, to charm the listening crowds
at some great festival); (2) on a passage of
clear, straightforward narrative,[9] the scholiast,
who is for once having an easy time in his den
of difficulties, facetiously exclaims, ' Here the
lion smiled! '[10] On the whole, the Greek schol-
iasts are disappointing, though they occasionally preserve something really valuable from
earlier and better sources. The *Life* of Thucydides, ascribed to a Marcellinus of uncertain
date, and (in its present form) perhaps not
earlier than the sixth century A.D., may for
convenience be grouped here; its remarks on
the style of Thucydides deserve careful attention.

To return for a moment to known scholars
of the Alexandrian age: we find some good lit-

erary criticism in Eratosthenes (the founder of scientific geography), as reported and criticized by Strabo who, two centuries later, wrote the most important work on ancient geography which has come down to us. Eratosthenes did not think it reasonable to demand minute geographical exactitude from the poet of the *Odyssey:* 'the aim of every poet,' said he, 'is to charm the mind, not to advance science'; [11] and again 'you will find the scene of Odysseus' wanderings when you find the cobbler who sewed up the bag of the winds.' [12] Strabo, with the traditional Greek reverence for the lessons found in the first of poets, regards Homer as the originator of geography, as well as of agriculture, generalship, rhetoric; and he chides the more imaginative Eratosthenes in the literal and prosaic spirit of Zoilus, the 'scourge of Homer,' who, somewhat before the Alexandrian age, had asked, in reference to the Ninth *Odyssey* (line 60), how it comes to pass that precisely *six* of Odysseus' men were slain from each several ship, adding that 'fictions ought at least to be plausible.'

Strabo makes amends for his ill-judged defence of Homer by his enthusiasm when he has later, in passing, to refer to Sappho: 'Sappho, a

marvellous creature; for, in all recorded time,
we know of no woman who has rivalled her (no,
not even in a small way) as a poet.'[13] And if
(as we have seen above) he regards Homer as
the founder of rhetoric, he is on safer ground
when he maintains that the art of poetry came
upon the scene sooner than the art of prose.[14]

In the vast collection of epigrams known as
the Greek Anthology, drawn from every quarter of the Greek-speaking world and ranging
over the seventeen centuries from 700 B.C. to
1000 A.D., some poetesses find a place. Among
them Nossis of Locri, who lived about 300 B.C.,
seems to contest the supremacy of Sappho.[15]
Against this rivalry by a woman must be set
the judgment of men in every age. Strabo, in
his eulogy, is clearly speaking for the world of
men; and Meleager, when weaving his chaplet
of song, describes Sappho's poems as ' few, but
roses all,' while Poseidippus says that her ' fair
pages yet remain and shall remain.'[16] One of
the best literary tributes of man to man is that
paid by Plato to Aristophanes, ' The Graces,
seeking to take a sanctuary that will not fall,
found the soul of Aristophanes.' This tribute
is preserved elsewhere than in the ancient
Greek Anthology, of whose contributions to

literary criticism it has been said that " Often we find in these epigrams some vivid epithet or fine image; in the ' frowning towers ' of the Aeschylean tragedy, the trumpet-note of Pindar, the wealth of lovely flower and leaf, crisp Acharnian ivy, rose and vine, that clusters round the tomb of Sophocles, there is a real touch of imaginative criticism." [17]

With this passing glance at some of the poets of a later and far-scattered Greece, we return to its prose authors. First may come Dio of Prusa in Bithynia, who flourished about 80 A.D. and was therefore, in the judgment of the present writer, a near contemporary of Demetrius and Longinus. Dio, in a passage already [18] referred to, looks back to Aristotle as the founder of literary criticism, remarking that ' Aristotle himself, with whom they say that the art of criticism and grammar originated, treats of the poet (Homer) in many dialogues, for the most part with admiration and honour.' [19] Together with his undoubted contemporary Plutarch, Dio is one of the finer Greek spirits of his time. Both of them revived some of the best features of the language, literature, and thought of the earlier Greece, and both had much true philosophy in them, untainted by the trivialities, insincerities, and ostentations of that sophistical rhetoric which Aristotle had once denounced, and which now again was flourishing in the larger Roman world. As regards criticism, a remarkable passage of Dio's is that of his twelfth 'oration' (or essay) in which Pheidias is made to contrast sculpture and poetry in some detail. As we read it, we are reminded of Simonides' famous saying (which Lessing quotes in the preface to his *Laokoon*) that 'painting is silent poetry, poetry is vocal painting.' Another passage is almost, if not quite, unique in Greek literature as a specimen of comparative criticism and appreciation: the passage in which the treatment by the three great Greek tragedians of the story of Philoctetes, left for many years on the island of Lemnos, is described with true dramatic insight and literary enjoyment.[20]

Dio of Prusa was, because of his eloquence, often called Dio Chrysostomus, 'Dio the Golden-mouthed.' The same title was, for the same reason, given three centuries later to the Christian Father, St. John Chrysostom. Chrysostom, who was a pupil of Libanius and was himself one of the greatest of Christian orators, speaks, in his treatise on the *Priesthood*, of

' the smoothness of Isocrates, the weight of Demosthenes, the dignity of Thucydides, and the elevation (sublimity) of Plato.' [21] Such literary labels are often misleading, but here they are well chosen and indicate taste and training. Among the Greek Fathers, Greek learning had been conspicuously possessed at an earlier date by Clement of Alexandria (160–215 A.D.), but it is theological rather than literary reasons that lead Clement to quote, and so to preserve for our industrial day, such a fragment as this of Sophocles:

> Go forth into the way, ye craftsmen all,
> Who supplicate, with winnowing fans aloft,
> The goddess Industry, stern child of Zeus. [22]

It is well thus briefly to remind ourselves that, among the early Christians, there were many writers, including St. Paul himself, who knew and appreciated ancient Greek literature, though concerning themselves little with formal rhetoric and literary criticism.

A younger contemporary of St. Paul's, Plutarch of Chaeroneia, is a profuse quoter from Greek literature, but he is no rhetorician, good or bad, and certainly no literary critic of the Aristotelian stamp. Being a moralist above all things, Plutarch follows without question the traditional Greek view that the chief aim of poetry is to mould character, whereas Aristotle holds (like Dryden long after him) that poetry is meant, above all, to give pleasure. Still there is, in the multifarious writings of a man who has been one of the world's best teachers, much that is of distinctively literary interest.

The extant *Lives* by Plutarch comprise those of Demosthenes and Cicero and a set 'comparison' between the two men. But, early in his *Demosthenes*, Plutarch makes it plain that, because he knows too little Latin, he will not attempt to compare the *speeches* of the two orators, but will examine their characters in the light of their conduct as *statesmen;* at the end of his *Cicero* he deftly introduces the tribute paid by Augustus to the Roman statesman many years after his death, ' An eloquent man, my boy; eloquent, and a lover of his country.' It is unfortunate that a few Greek men of letters, like Sophocles or Aeschylus, are not the subject of Plutarch's skill as a biographer. Three Boeotian *Lives* are said to have perished, and to have included not only the man of action, Epameinondas, but (standing perhaps in a class apart) the poets Hesiod and Pindar.

Plutarch's other, and very miscellaneous, writings would, to-day, still more appropriately than the orations of Dio, be called 'Essays.' Their traditional Latin title is *Moralia*, or moral writings. This name well describes their general trend, for, as Emerson said, Plutarch is, above all things, 'a chief example of the illumination of the intellect by the force of morals.' [23] His vast influence is, in fact, due to his own character and his lively sense of character in others, — to his broad and genial humanity. In some of the essays, literary questions arise, as the main subject or incidentally. For example, the heading 'Comparison between Aristophanes and Menander' might suggest a purely literary treatment. But Plutarch sees a grossness in Aristophanes which blinds him to his genius and leads him to award the palm to the judicious Menander. At the same time this essay — or epitome of an essay — would repay a more detailed study than it has hitherto received, or than can be given to it here; its very faults are instructive. One of its faults is the lack of a true historic sense. Plutarch seems to take no account of the social conditions under which the boisterous Old Attic Comedy lived and throve. Though himself a faithful citizen of a little Greek town, he lived at a time when the local and national characteristics of the past were apt to be forgotten in the vague cosmopolitanism of the present. He forgets, for instance, that the Homeric age was a long way back and that, when Homer, as the traditional Greek teacher of morality, is not quite on his loftiest plane, it is better to think of the early times in which he wrote than to force his words into all sorts of fantastic meanings. On the other hand, we occasionally find in Plutarch a bit of reported criticism which bears the stamp of truth upon it, such as Sophocles' estimate of the three phases of his own poetic style: an estimate which should be checked by a careful modern study of the surviving plays and fragments, and of Plutarch's scattered allusions to all three tragedians.[24] Among his more general observations of a literary kind is the important one that the hearer (or, as we should say, the reader) has a duty to perform as well as the speaker (or writer); there should be a rhythmical accord between the two, as in a well-played game of ball.[25] Good, again, is the protest (having a pleasant quaintness of its own in the translation edited by Doctor Philemon Holland) against the dilettante's attention to

style and neglect of substance: ' As for those
that read the books of Plato and Xenophon in
no other regard but for the beauty of their gal-
lant style, seeking for nought else but for the
purity of speech and the very natural Attic
language, as if they went to gather the thin dew
or tender moss or down of herbs; What shall
you say of such? ' [26] In the tract *On the Malig-
nity of Herodotus,* doubtfully attributed to Plutarch, the attractive style of Herodotus is duly
praised, but habitual unfairness in political
criticism is alleged against him. If Plutarch be
the author, the Boeotian in him is revolting
against Herodotean reflections on Boeotian
policy during the Persian War. Whoever the
author may be, the essay contains little that can
be regarded as literary criticism, and much
that shows an imperfect sense of the austere
standards of history.

To Epictetus, the Stoic philosopher and contemporary of Plutarch, eloquence is no more
than one of life's inns, pleasant only as a house
of passage. But Epictetus can himself rise to
the religious eloquence of a prose hymn, when
he offers thanks for the blessing of life: ' Now
it is Thy will for me to leave the festival. I go,
giving all thanks to Thee, that Thou didst deign

to let me share Thy festival and see Thy works and understand Thy government.'²⁷ Marcus Aurelius, somewhat later than Epictetus and much influenced by him, has learnt with gratitude, from the Stoic philosopher Rusticus to 'eschew rhetoric and poetry and fine language.'²⁸ This distrust of ornamental language was a marked trait in the Stoics, and was good when it sprang from the love of unvarnished truth, bad when it was prompted by the fear of self-pleasing. When the young Marcus confesses this fear to his tutor Fronto, Fronto rightly asks him: 'Why not cure your vanity rather than renounce its cause?' Marcus may have taken the counsel to heart later. In the acquired Greek of his 'Inmost Thoughts,' the style is better and easier as time goes on. Of literary criticism, a useful fragment is found in XI. §6: 'Tragedy, the first form of drama, drew its lessons from experience, partly as true to the facts of existence, and partly to take the sting, upon the larger stage of life, from things which appeal to the emotions on the stage. . . . After tragedy came the old comedy, reprimanding like a schoolmaster, and in its bluff outspoken way usefully rebuking pride; somewhat in the style of like deliverances by Diogenes.

Next understand the meaning of middle comedy, and finally of the new comedy, noting to what ends it was applied and how it gradually degenerated into mere mimic diversion. That some good things occur even here, every one knows; but what was the main object and aim of that school of poetry and drama?' [29] Galen, the family physician of Marcus and an indefatigable writer on medical and philosophical subjects, is known to have dealt, more than once, with ancient comedy, and in all his writing to have kept in mind the Aristotelian view that clearness is the greatest merit of style.[30]

Lucian the Syrian,[30a] another contemporary of Marcus Aurelius, was not only a student of ancient comedy, but a zealous imitator of its easy, witty, brilliant style: the style of Aristophanes at his best, and of Plato at his best. Trained by, and living among, the showy 'Sophists' of his day, he proves his independence and his inborn taste by counting their airs and graces as dross beside the works of the great classic exemplars. He never tires of quoting Homer or alluding to him. Among philosophers, Plato seems to be his favourite; among historians, Thucydides; in the drama, Euripides and Aristophanes rather than

Aeschylus or Sophocles; in oratory, Demosthenes. In his *True History* he mocks, as a master of parody and burlesque, at the wild and fabulous stories in which the chroniclers of ' mendacious Greece ' were supposed to delight. His *How to Write History* is no detailed handbook for the historian, but it does him a better service; it sets before him a noble ideal of his office, and sends him to Thucydides as a model of historical truth-telling. This remarkable passage should be read in full.[31] Its burden is that the ideal historian will be marked by truthfulness, intelligence, power of expression; he will, in fact, cultivate alike science and art. The faults and affectations of contemporary rhetoricians, or sophists, are satirized not only in this essay but in the *Professor of Rhetoric* and (incidentally) in the *Parasite,* while the *Lexiphanes* exposes to ridicule those ' Atticists ' of the day who showed pedantry in their extravagant devotion to the old Attic dialect and were strangers to the taste and discrimination with which Lucian used it in his own writings. It is the same good taste that has made him, by common consent, one of the very best art-critics of antiquity. Towards the end of the *Lexiphanes,* he gives sound advice to the man who would speak, or write, well: he must imitate not the modern sophists but the classical models; he must beware 'the windflowers of speech'; he must be like an athlete in training; he must sacrifice to the Graces and to Lucidity.

Hermogenes of Tarsus, though contemporary with Lucian, is an author of a very different kind. Trained in the fashionable rhetoric of the day, Lucian soon left its narrow paths for the great highways of Homeric and Attic literature, and for the inspiration which could still be found on them by writers who had themselves something to say. Hermogenes developed, while still a boy-prodigy admired by Marcus Aurelius, an elaborate system of technical rhetoric, highly ingenious but spoilt by fine, wire-drawn, hair-splitting, never-ending distinctions. It is this type of arid, terminological, over-subtle, over-analytical rhetoric, with minute distinctions ever more far-fetched and absurd, and with technical rules that are often trivial and lifeless and soulless, that was passed on from Hermogenes to a host of followers and commentators, and through them to later ages. 'Rhetoric' has thus often deserved to be a mere byword, except when a superior mind, like that of St. Augustine, has reverted to some

really great master of the craft like Cicero.[32]
It may be regarded as significant that in Hermogenes' writings the name of Aristotle never
once occurs. On the other hand, it is to his
credit that, among orators, he has a great admiration for Demosthenes, and, among poets,
for Homer. He shares with other rhetoricians
the tendency to regard history as a mere branch
of rhetoric or panegyric, but his respect for
Thucydides is a good point in him as in Lucian.
Still, the fact remains that he has not that keen
appreciation of literature for its own sake which
belongs to Lucian and which prompts Dionysius, or Longinus, to transcribe odes of Sappho. Nor is this appreciation conspicuous in a
number of later rhetoricians, or sophists, who
call for a passing mention and whose names
may be given in rough chronological order: (1)
Aristeides [32a] of Smyrna (170 A.D.: so a contemporary of Hermogenes rather than a successor)
was famous, in his own day and long afterwards,
as a speech-writer who imitated diligently the
old Attic models and Demosthenes above all.
He may be classed with those salaried professors who abounded under the Antonines; but he
must not be identified with ' Aristeides the rhetorician ' whose ' seven pupils, four walls and

three benches ' are mentioned ironically in one of the epigrams (XI.162) of the Greek Anthology; (2) Maximus of Tyre (180 A.D.) is more given to the study of philosophy, Plato especially, than is Aristeides; in his way of writing he shows the excess of symmetry, and the other mannerisms, which afflicted Greek prose composition from the days of Gorgias; (3) Philostratus of Athens (210 A.D.) wrote the *Lives of the Sophists,* a collection which includes alike the ancient sophists (among them, Gorgias) and the ' new sophists ' of his own and slightly earlier times. Philostratus lived in a century when poetry and science had sunk low but the star of romance was rising steadily. To the modern reader his writings present two special points of interest: he offers a formal definition of the Greek word ' phantasia ' which shows that by his time the idea of creative imagination in its modern sense had been largely anticipated by writers with a critical bent, and he supplies the fabric out of which Ben Jonson wove his well-known *Song to Celia,* ' Drink to me only with thine eyes '; (4) in the latter half of the fourth century may be grouped the rhetoricians Themistius, Libanius, Himerius, and Eunapius; and then, or earlier,

comes the Menander who distinguished as many
as twenty-seven types of epideictic discourse.
Of Libanius it has been said that 'he speaks
from books and like a book'; but he was not
wholly bookish or he would not have been a fit
teacher for his pupil Chrysostom nor have left
us that vivid picture of students who at Athens
or Antioch, as sometimes in later universities,
tried to put their teacher out of countenance by
ostentatiously folding their arms or staring at
the trees outside.

Fragmentary traces of rhetorical lore or of
elementary literary criticism may also be found
in men who were not professed rhetoricians or
critics. Athenaeus of Naucratis (c.225 A.D.),
in that antiquarian haggis called the *Deipno-*
sophistae, or *Professors at Dinner*, ranges over
the most miscellaneous topics which can in any
way be connected with the pleasures of the
table. His mental calibre is that of a scholiast
rather than of a literary critic, but he furnishes
profuse materials of which, fragmentary though
they are, literary criticism and literary history
must take account. He quotes, thanks to the
efficiency of the Alexandrian Library, from as
many as seven hundred Greek authors now
lost; the remains of the Middle and New Attic

Comedy come to us very largely through him;
he has preserved the famous poem of Callistra-
tus on Harmodius and Aristogeiton. A little
later in the same century may be placed two
writers, Plotinus and Diogenes Laertius, whose
names have philosophical rather than purely
literary associations. Plotinus, the foremost
of Neo-Platonists, tried to find a better meta-
physical basis for art than Plato himself had
recognized. Diogenes Laertius, in his uncritical
attempt to write a general history of Greek
philosophy, is often led, incidentally, to speak
of the study of rhetoric.

In the fourth century Greek prose literature
may be regarded as coming to an end with the
death of Julian: true poetry had long been dead.
Julian was at once emperor, sophist, and apostate. ' Sophist ' reminds us of a characteristic
and persistent side of Greek literary activity;
' apostate,' of the spread of Christian influence
when, with the seat of empire now removed to
Constantinople, a Roman emperor could be
branded with the Greek name for ' renegade.'
In attacking Christianity, Julian makes a striking remark about the peoples of the West:
' With very few exceptions, you will not find
that the men of the Western nations have any

great inclination for philosophy or geometry or studies of that sort, although the Roman Empire has now so long been paramount. Those who are unusually talented delight only in debate or the art of rhetoric, and do not adopt any other study.' [33]

Perhaps Ausonius, who during this same century was, so to say, Professor of Latin and Greek Rhetoric in the University of Bordeaux, may be thought to confirm Julian's statement. Though nothing of a philosopher or mathematician, Ausonius was something of a poet, as his *Mosella* shows. But most of his poetry, or verse, has a rhetorical cast; and he may be regarded as a professorial harbinger of that rhetoric, too often frivolous, which was to spread widely among the younger nations of the Western world.[34]

VI. 'LONGINUS ON THE SUBLIME'

WHILE retaining for convenience the traditional title of this famous treatise, the present writer feels even more convinced than he was when he edited it in the year 1899 that it cannot be assigned to the third century of our era and (in that century) to the historical Longinus, the 'living library and walking university,' who, as the minister of Zenobia, Queen of Palmyra, bravely met his death at Aurelian's hands. There is no space here to review or supplement the arguments on either side; it can only be said that, as far as external evidence goes, the author of the treatise must be regarded as unidentified, while its actual contents point strongly to the first century as the date of composition.

The treatise (or essay, rather) opens with a reference to a tract on the same subject — ' the Sublime ' — by a certain Caecilius. Caecilius was, as we have seen in Chapter IV, a contemporary and friend of Dionysius of Halicarnas-

sus, and like him taught rhetoric at Rome in the
time of Augustus. The polemical tone of 'Longinus,' when he mentions Caecilius both at the
beginning and elsewhere, makes it natural to
suppose that he follows him at no long interval
of time and belongs to a rival school among the
Greek critics of the day. We may, therefore,
assign him and his work, conjecturally, to a
date not far from the year 40 A.D.,[1] and may
also observe that, while Dionysius finds his
masters specially in the Attic Orators (Lysias,
Isocrates, and the rest) and Demetrius depends
largely on the teachings of Aristotle and Theophrastus, 'Longinus' seeks his inspiration in
Plato, and is himself, centuries later, in the
thick of that fray between Plato and the pro-
fessional orators such as Lysias, which is described in Chapter I of this book.

Let us briefly sketch the general contents of
the essay, and then single out a few points of
special interest. Its broad aim is to indicate the
essential elements of an elevated style, which,
avoiding turgidity, puerility, affectation and bad
taste, finds its inspiration in great thought and
deep emotion, and its expression in a noble diction and a well ordered composition; it is, in
effect, a short essay in literary criticism, with

[123]

special reference to distinction of style. Its author begins thus: 'You will remember, my dear Postumius Terentianus, that when we examined together the treatise of Caecilius on the Sublime, we found that it fell below the dignity of the whole subject, while it failed signally to grasp the essential points, and conveyed to its readers but little of that practical help which it should be a writer's principal aim to give.' The name of the Roman pupil here addressed is not altogether clear in the oldest manuscript, and we can hardly say more about him than that he seems to have been a person of official rank. The 'practical help' which Caecilius had failed to offer is the due consideration of 'the means whereby we may raise our own capacities to the right pitch of elevation.' Sublimity itself is, in the course of the first chapter, described as a certain loftiness and excellence of language; it is, we are told, through their sublimity that the greatest authors in poetry and prose have reached the foremost place and gained immortal renown. Sublimity has a power unknown to that kind of writing, or speaking, which simply persuades or pleases; it transports and masters us in ways that are beyond the reach of mere technical skill.

The second chapter asks one of those far-reaching questions which the author is in the habit of raising. Is there an *art* of sublimity, when sublimity might seem to be just a natural gift, and as such unteachable? The answer given is that Nature herself does not work at random, and the greatest natural forces are most in need of such control and guidance as can be devised by man; Nature stands first, Art second, but both are essential. Besides, how is the critic to gauge natural genius except by the aid of Art?

At this point comes one of those six or seven gaps in the Greek text of the essay which, taken together, have reduced it to three-fifths of its original length, till some fortunate discovery restores the missing portions. When the text resumes, the author is discussing vices of style which result from disastrous attempts to be sublime: turgidity, puerility, and the like. All these faults arise from 'that pursuit of novelty in the expression of ideas which may be regarded as the fashionable craze of our day.' A thought is not truly sublime if it does not bear repetition; if it does not implant itself ineradicably in the memory; if it does not uplift us time after time; if it speedily falls flat. The

[125]

verdict of all men through all ages must be accepted as final. Writings that can stand such searching tests as these are the classics of literature. As for the critic, his task is no easy one, since '*literary criticism* is the last and crowning fruit of long experience.'[2]

Then follows a list of five sources of sublime, or elevated, style; and an inquiry into these five sources forms the basis of the rest of the essay, with however many digressions on subsidiary topics and no rigid adherence to the main grouping. Of the five sources two are mainly innate, namely: (1) 'the power of forming great conceptions' and (2) 'vehement and inspired passion,' while the remaining three are the result rather of art; (3) the 'figures' of thought and language; (4) 'noble diction'; (5) 'dignified and elevated composition.' In other words you must think greatly; feel deeply; shape your thoughts and language effectively; choose words beautiful in themselves and in their associations; arrange your words and thoughts with dignity and impressiveness.

The ninth chapter opens with a characteristic passage: " Now the first of these sources, natural greatness, holds the foremost rank among them all. We must, therefore, although we have here to do with an endowment rather than with an acquirement, nurture our souls (so far as that is possible) to all that is great, and make them always pregnant, so to say, with noble inspiration. In what way, you may ask, is this to be done? Elsewhere I have written as follows: ' Sublimity is the echo of a great soul ' (or, in the author's elaborate language, ' the reverberation of magnanimity '). Hence also a bare idea, by itself and without a spoken word, sometimes wins admiration just because it betokens greatness of soul. Thus the silence of Ajax in the book of the Underworld is great and more sublime than any speech. . . . The true orator must be free from low and ignoble thoughts. For it is not possible that men with mean and servile ideas and aims prevailing throughout their lives should produce anything that is admirable and worthy of immortality." It is at this point that the longest gap in the essay occurs. After it, the author is still dealing with the first source and still drawing illustrations of it from the great Homeric store, with which he links for a moment the Hebrew Bible in a Greek rendering: " Similarly, the legislator of the Jews, no ordinary man, having formed and expressed a worthy conception of the might of the Godhead, writes at the very beginning of his Laws, ' God said ' — what? ' Let there be light: and there was light; let there be earth: and there was earth.' " This quotation, which surely comes from the original writer and from no later interpolator, follows upon Homeric passages in which the divine power is described, — the divine greatness and purity, and the divine control over the elements. It is itself followed by a reference to the deeds and thoughts of *men,* as depicted in Homer: in particular, the famous prayer of Ajax in the Seventeenth *Iliad,* when the battlefield of the Greeks is suddenly shrouded by mist and baffling night, and the hero, at his wits' end, cries to Father Zeus to save the sons of the Achaeans from beneath the gloom. ' Make thou clear day; grant us to see with our eyes; and if thou must slay, slay in the light! ' This leads on to what the author himself describes as a ' digression,' a striking comparison between the *Iliad* and the *Odyssey.* It is clear, we are told, that Homer wrote the *Odyssey* later than the *Iliad,* and when his powers were declining; it is simply an epilogue to the *Iliad,* doing honour to the dead heroes of the Trojan war and to some of its minor episodes; the *Iliad* was written at the

[128]

height of his inspiration and is full of action and conflict, while the *Odyssey* for the most part consists of narrative, as is characteristic of old age; in the *Odyssey* Homer may be likened to the setting sun whose grandeur remains without its intensity or to the ebb of some great tidal waters; throughout the *Odyssey* the fabulous element prevails over the real, and the decline in the passion of the writer's prime is accompanied by an enhanced interest in details of personal character, so that the sketches of daily life in the household of Odysseus resemble a comedy of manners. But ' if I speak of old age, it is nevertheless the old age of Homer.'

The author shows next, by means of some famous examples drawn from the best Greek literature, how great thoughts should be selected skilfully and combined into an organic whole or (his other image) into a building which, however small, is wrought in solid masonry, being composed of large blocks so well dressed and fitted as to need little mortar or none. Thus does Homer portray a storm, Archilochus a shipwreck, Demosthenes the bringing to Athens of the news that Elateia had been taken, and Sappho the feelings of frenzied love, as described in the *Ode to Anactoria* (preserved here only), where we see ' not one passion only, but a concourse of the passions.'

Under the heading of the first source is also discussed the use of ' amplification ' (or the gradual enhancing of a thought) and of imagery. Another digression here compares Plato with Demosthenes, and Demosthenes with the Roman Cicero. Plato, it is pointed out, was a devoted student of Homer, and as a writer entered the lists, so to say, against him in healthy rivalry. So should we minor writers think how Homer, Plato, or Demosthenes would have put this thing or that; nay more, ' in what spirit all the ages after me will listen to me who have written thus,' an alarming prospect, but one from which an author must not shrink!

At this point we expect to find, as the second ' source,' the question of the Passions or Emotions. These, however, are not separately treated in the *Sublime*, though at the end of Chapter XLIV the author says that he had previously promised to write a special essay upon them; and he seems about to redeem his promise when his book breaks off suddenly with an unfinished sentence. But throughout the existing work he stresses, incidentally, the importance of giving full play to the emotions under proper control and direction. Nowhere is this view more strongly pressed than when he is dealing with rhetorical technicalities, such as those ' figures ' which form the third ' source ' and had been treated by previous writers in wearisome and interminable detail. ' A figure is at its best when the very fact that it is a figure escapes attention. Accordingly, sublimity and emotion form an antidote and a wonderful help against the mistrust which attends upon the use of figures.' [3] Similarly he says later, with regard to metaphors and not without peril to his pupils, that ' the proper time for using metaphors is when the emotions roll like a torrent and sweep a multitude of them down their resistless flood.' [4] Among the Figures explained and illustrated by him are adjuration; rhetorical question; asyndeton; hyperbaton; interchanges of grammatical cases, numbers, tenses, persons, genders; periphrasis.[5]

The treatment of the fourth ' source ' — Diction — has hardly begun when we are confronted with the second-largest gap in the essay. Before it occurs, however, the author has said, in memorable terms, that ' the choice of the right words and of grand words wonderfully attracts and enthrals the hearer, and such a

choice is the chief study of all speakers and
writers, since this of itself brings to literature,
as though to the fairest sculpture, greatness,
beauty, mellowness, weight, force, strength,
and a certain brilliance, and breathes into dead
things a kind of living voice. Beautiful words
are in very truth the peculiar light of thought.' [6]
After the lacuna, Caecilius is being taken to task
for condemning certain homely expressions
which are justified by their vigour, and also for
limiting unduly the number of metaphors which
may be used together in the same passage.
Plato sometimes uses metaphors in excess, and
in this he is wrong. But we must not, for that
reason, follow Caecilius in preferring to Plato
the flawless Lysias.[7] Which, in general, are we
to place first, — greatness with attendant faults,
or a faultlessness which lacks greatness? Or a
number of claims to excellence rather than one
supreme claim? Surely there can be no doubt
as between Homer and Apollonius, Pindar and
Bacchylides, Sophocles and Ion, Demosthenes
and Hypereides, or lastly Plato and Lysias.[8] It
is in connexion with these two last writers that
the author is moved to make a highly characteristic declaration: ' What fact, then, (he asks)
was before the eyes of those superhuman writ-

ers (Plato, as contrasted with Lysias, is chiefly meant) who, aiming at the greatest things in authorship, thought little of an all-pervading correctitude? This besides much else, that Nature has appointed us men to be no low or ignoble animals; but when she ushers us into life and into the vast universe as into some great assembly, to be as it were spectators of the mighty whole and the keenest aspirants for honour, forthwith she implants in our souls the unconquerable love of whatever is great and more divine than we. Wherefore not even the entire universe suffices for the thought and contemplation within the reach of the human mind, but our imaginations often pass beyond the bounds of space, and if we survey our life on every side and see how much more it every-where abounds in what is striking, and great, and beautiful, we shall soon discern the pur-pose of our birth. This is why, by a sort of natural impulse, we admire not the small streams, useful and pellucid though they be, but the Nile, the Danube, or the Rhine, and still more the Ocean. Nor do we view the tiny flame of our own kindling, clear and steady as its light well may be, with greater awe than the celestial fires though they are often shrouded in darkness; nor do we deem it a greater marvel than the craters of Etna, whose eruptions throw up stones from its depths and great masses of rock, and at times pour forth rivers of that pure and unalloyed fire which is beneath the earth.' [9] As regards literature, the conclusion of the whole matter here is: it is sublimity, rather than faultlessness, that lifts men near to the majesty of God. And if we are told that a faulty statue is not redeemed by its size, we answer that in Art correctness comes first, in Nature greatness; and language is a natural gift. But Art is needed as an aid to Nature; and it is when the two are found working hand in hand that we may look for perfection.[10]

After this long and inspiring digression, similes and the like are beginning to be discussed (in connexion with the subject of metaphor) when another gap occurs, at the end of which hyperbole is under consideration as the last item in the section dealing with diction.[11]

Then comes the fifth source: the due arrangement of words and phrases in good writing. That is the special meaning of the word *synthesis* in Greek, as we have seen in the work of Dionysius described on pages 85–97 above. But Dionysius' book takes so wide a range that

we have found it convenient to English its title
as *On Literary Composition,* and so to include
the selection not only of words but of those ideas
from which words can hardly be kept entirely
apart. The author of the *Sublime* had, he tells
us (c.39), himself written two tracts on composition. These have not come down to us, and
here he is content to illustrate his views from
Demosthenes and Euripides, and to call attention, under this head, to such defects as excess
of rhythm, broken and jerky clauses, undue
condensation and undue diffuseness, and finally
all words and combinations of words that are
trivial and vulgar.[12]

In his concluding chapter (c.44) the author
laments the dearth of great oratory in his own
age, an age in which, he says, there was talent
enough but no genius; and he finds the cause
not so much in the loss of political freedom as
in moral decay. The passage has a bearing on
the approximate date of the essay. No dirge
of the kind is found in similar writings subse-
quent to the first century — in Lucian, or Aristeides, or Maximus of Tyre. In the first
century, on the other hand, the topic was a hackneyed one, as this chapter tells us, and as we can
ourselves infer from surviving Latin authors:

[135]

from various passages in Tacitus, the two
Plinys, the two Senecas, Petronius, Quintilian;
or, among Greek writers, Philo and Plutarch.
Within the first century, complaints of the kind
might be found at almost any time; and so
might references, in one form or another, to
'the world's peace.'[13]

At whatever date we place the *Sublime,* we
must not fall into the error of regarding it as
an isolated work. It is apt to appear so to us
because the tract of Caecilius to which it is a
reply has been lost. But both the author himself and Caecilius had written much in the field
of literary criticism, and in the first century A.D.
there were assuredly many other Greek literary critics whose works may yet be recovered
by modern excavation. The distinction of
'Longinus' is not that he stands alone but that
he is himself. From his first page to his last
you feel that you are listening to no mere echo
but to a living voice. And this deep impression
of personality is the more remarkable because
of that wide range of outlook and reflexion
which might easily have dimmed it. He has historical vista, and sweeps the centuries from
Homer to the Alexandrians and to Caecilius
himself, dispensing praise and blame with fear-

less and impartial hand to writers alike of prose
and verse. He is comparative and interna-
tional; in no other Greek writer do we find a literary criticism which embraces both Cicero
and Moses and can (while thinking but little of
Alexandrian Greek writers) discern greatness in
the new literature of Rome and in the ancient
literature of despised Judaea. In all literature
he seems to see the reflexion of individual and
national life; beneath great writing he thinks he
finds some great human spirit. To quote again
words in which his fine egotism declares itself:
"Elsewhere I have written as follows: 'Sublimity is the echo of a great soul.' . . . The
true orator must be free from low and ignoble
thoughts. For it is not possible that men with
mean and servile ideas and aims prevailing
throughout their lives should produce anything
that is admirable and worthy of immortality."
Vir bonus dicendi peritus! He feels that the
test of really great literature is its sublimity or
'height'; and, like Matthew Arnold, he sees in
it the high seriousness which comes from absolute sincerity. As for the final court of appeal, he would put his trust (as we have seen)
in the united judgment of mankind: 'In general, consider those sublimities to be fine and

[137]

genuine which please always, and please all.
For when men who differ in their pursuits, lives,
ambitions, age, speech, hold identical views on
one and the same subject, then that verdict
which results, so to speak, from a concert of
discordant elements, makes our faith in the object of admiration strong and unassailable.' [14]
No modern critic could formulate more precisely, in relation to the classics of all eras and
all nations, the *quod semper, quod ubique* principle.

VII. INFLUENCE

THE influence of Greek rhetoric and literary criticism, in Roman and later times, will have suggested itself in every previous chapter: the very words 'rhetoric' and 'criticism' tell their own tale. In this concluding chapter some main streams of far-flowing influence may be indicated. It will be well to begin with 'Longinus,' to take Dionysius next, and to end with Demetrius. As these three writers all lived in the days of Rome, they will, like bridges, help us to look both backwards and forwards; and with each we shall connect an outstanding name in the great age of Greece.

Longinus carries us back to Plato and that early feud between philosophy and rhetoric which finds echoes as late as the time of Aristeides who can, in the second century A.D., engage in a refutation of Plato's *Gorgias*. Longinus himself speaks of rhetoricians, and their idol Isocrates, with some disdain. Even of the philosophers Aristotle and Theophrastus he

makes but a passing mention. It is Plato that
he regards as the great model of 'sublimity' in
prose, though he does not fail to criticize him
when there is need. From Plato he quotes, as
typical, that passage of the *Republic* in which
we are told that 'those who are destitute of
wisdom and goodness . . . never look upwards
to the truth, nor do they lift their heads on high,
nor enjoy any pure and lasting pleasure, but
like unto the beasts of the field they have their
eyes ever cast downwards and bent upon the
ground and upon their dining-tables.'[1] It is this
moral elevation that draws him to Plato: the
feeling, shared by Plato and Dante, that ' Fatti
non foste a viver come bruti, Ma per seguir
virtute e conoscenza.'[2] In form as well as spirit
the passage may be regarded as typical not only
of Plato but of Longinus, — in the rhythm of
the clauses and the semi-poetical use of the word
translated 'like unto.' Altogether it has that
high literary excellence which Plato possessed,
but disparaged — even when found in the greatest poetry of his race. While Longinus shares
to-day in the general vitality of Platonism, as a
critic he is superior to his master in that he
frankly delights in literature as literature and
finds in Plato's own writings an ever-fresh

spring of inspiration and of an unfailing sublimity. Among our own poet-critics it is Pope
— the apostle of correctitude — who, in his
Essay on Criticism, has best appraised
Longinus:

Thee, bold Longinus! all the Nine inspire,
And bless their Critic with a Poet's fire.
An ardent Judge, who zealous in his trust,
With warmth gives sentence, yet is always just;
Whose own example strengthens all his laws;
And is himself that great Sublime he draws.

Among our great writers of prose, Gibbon says
that, when criticizing a beautiful passage,
Longinus ' tells me his own feelings; and tells
them with such energy, that he communicates
them. I almost doubt which is most sublime,
Homer's Battle of the Gods, or Longinus' apos-
trophe to Terentianus upon it.' Milton, too, in
his *Tractate of Education,* includes Longinus
among those authors from whom should be
learnt ' a graceful and ornate rhetoric, taught
out of the rule of Plato, Aristotle, Phalereus,
Cicero, Hermogenes, Longinus.' In the preceding sentence, Milton speaks of ' the fitted style
of lofty, mean, or lowly.' This threefold division illustrates the long, but not easily traced,

influence of Greek rhetoric and literary criticism. In a Greek form, the division is not found earlier than Dionysius of Halicarnassus, whose three classes are named 'lofty' (the same word as in Longinus is translated by 'sublime'), 'plain,' and 'intermediate.' But, once more, we have to remember the almost total loss of Greek literature between Aristotle and Dionysius. Even in Aristotle's time it seems not unlikely that some such classification was current, since he deprecates, as we have seen, the application of the term 'magnificent' to style. 'Magnificent' is, more or less, akin to 'lofty,' and Aristotle's own definition of good style in the *Rhetoric* forbids alike too much and too little ornament and commends the good taste which steers a middle course. The *Rhetorica ad Herennium* (c.85 B.C.), and Cicero's *De Oratore* (55 B.C.) and *Orator* (c.45 B.C.), doubtless have Greek precedents behind them when, with that variety of terminology which is only natural in dealing with so intangible a matter as style, they present, in Latin, a triple division akin to that of Dionysius.[3]

Two passages of Dionysius seem to throw light on the history and meaning of ὕψος, *hupsos*, (if we may write the Greek term for

'loftiness' or 'sublimity' in English characters, as Dean Swift does): (1) 'Lofty and magnificent the style of Lysias is not'; (2) 'I shall
quote as examples of his [Plato's] vaunted
'lofty' style passages from one of his celebrated books' (*De Lys.* xiii; *ad Pomp.* ii. 9).
From both these passages it would appear that
the expression 'lofty,' or 'sublime,' was well
known to Dionysius (the contemporary, be it
remembered, of Caecilius) as marking the
quality which distinguished Plato from Lysias.
How long it had been in use, we cannot say.
Neither the adjective *sublimis,* which afterwards became the regular equivalent of the
Greek term, nor the corresponding noun *sub-
limitas,* is found in the writings of Cicero, who
was some forty years senior to Dionysius.
When Chaucer refers to the 'heigh style,' behind his epithet there lies no doubt, in some
unexplored way, the Latin *sublimis* and the corresponding Greek term.[4] The essay on the *Sublime* seems, so far as our evidence goes, to have
remained in obscurity from the time at which
it was written till the year 1554, when it was
printed for the first time, at Basle, by the
Italian Robortello who describes it (in Latin)
as 'a work previously unknown[5] and now

come to life again,' and as 'liber de grandi sive sublimi orationis genere.' The first English translation is that by John Hall: 'Dionysius Longinus of the Height of Eloquence rendered out of the originall,' London, 1652; the first French translation that by Boileau: 'Traité du sublime ou du merveilleux dans le discours. Traduit du grec de Longin,' Paris, 1674. The influence of Boileau gave great vogue to the essay (as a piece of *belles lettres* which every man of culture must know) not only in France but in England. In England alone, during the eighteenth and the last quarter of the seventeenth century, it can be shown to have been quoted, or mentioned with appreciation, by some fifty or sixty English writers, including men as notable as Addison, Dryden, Fielding, Gibbon, Goldsmith, Hurd, Johnson, Pope, Prior, Reynolds, Steele, Sterne, Swift, Warburton, Warton.[6] And, by what Johnson called a *Gallicism*, Boileau's 'sublime' became accepted as part of the title, in England as well as in France.

In Pope's critical theory, as in Boileau's, Longinus held a high place as the champion of a classic excellence. During the 'Romantic movement,' and for the greater part of the nineteenth century, he was somewhat neglected; but during the last thirty years there have been many signs of reawakened interest in him in England, America, and throughout Europe. Within the last few years he has been freshly translated into English, French, German, Italian, Modern Greek, and other languages: a sure sign that he still makes his appeal not only to professed scholars but to the wider circle of those who love great literature and like to hear it judged worthily by a worthy judge.

Dionysius, as his *First Letter to Ammaeus* shows, resents the exaggerated claims made in his day for the rhetoric of the philosophers (Aristotle especially), and is eager to prove how much the art also owes to orators, or oratorical writers, such as Isocrates. Like Isocrates, Dionysius delights in calling his own rhetoric ' philosophical '; but neither he nor Isocrates has that sweep of intellect which enables Aristotle to undertake a scientific treatment of the subject in all its bearings. A generation before Dionysius, Cicero had been a follower of Isocrates, but he endeavours, with characteristic eclecticism, to combine the system of Isocrates with that of Aristotle. To the following century — the first century A.D. — the present

writer would assign both Longinus and Demetrius, and would see a follower of Plato in the
one, of Aristotle and Theophrastus in the
other, and in neither of them any subservience
to Isocrates. In the second century A.D., we
find in Aristeides, and (to a large extent) in the
Second Sophistic generally, an Isocratic rhetoric which was to have great influence in all
succeeding ages. Influential through the direct
precepts contained in his pamphlets, Milton's
' old man eloquent ' has been still more influential through the example he set in his own careful and elaborate prose. As a prose-writer,
Isocrates (with his characteristic rhythm and
period) has, largely through the medium of
Cicero, helped to shape much of the oratorical
and literary prose of Europe: Bossuet, Milton
(in his *Areopagitica*), Jeremy Taylor, Edmund
Burke, John Ruskin.

As we have seen above (pp. 74, 75), certain
weaknesses in Isocrates' style are frankly indicated by Dionysius: he is no blind admirer of
him. And he is himself a literary critic far
beyond the measure of men like Isocrates and
Aristeides, neither of whom shows his familiarity with the great poets of Greece, whose
beauties he discerns and can make others dis-

cern. As Pope has it in his already-quoted
Essay on Criticism,

> See *Dionysius Homer's thoughts refine,*
> And *call new beauties forth from every line.*

Pope is thinking of various chapters in Dionysius' *Literary Composition,* while Tennyson,
in a letter written a full century later, shows
that he has been studying the surviving fragments of Alcaeus and Simonides in the light of a
summary we possess of a lost work by Dionysius on the literary characteristics of Greek
writers generally. As further illustrating the
long tradition of Greek study and literary appreciation, we may recall that a famous passage
of the *Odyssey* (xi.595–8) was admired, for
identical reasons, not only by Pope under
Queen Anne but, in the time of our Norman
Kings, by Eustathius (Archbishop of Thes-
salonica, 1175–1190), who writes that Homer's
very language here ' moves reluctantly, in keeping with the laboriousness of the heavy heave
uphill '; and, centuries before Eustathius, by
Dionysius and Demetrius.[7]

Like Longinus and Dionysius, Demetrius is
a convenient Greek bridge (of Roman date)
between past and present. It would be tedious

and unnecessary to give detailed evidence, or illustration, of Roman indebtedness to Aristotle. As might be expected, the greater the writer and reasoner the greater is his respect for 'the master of those that know': we see this in Cicero, Quintilian, St. Augustine, and Boethius.[8] Among lesser Greek and Roman writers the inferior, or scholastic and 'sophistical,' type of rhetoric prevailed and came to form part of the 'Trivium,' which also included logic and grammar. The supremacy of Aristotle was gradually established in England, after the printing, by Aldus Manutius at Venice in 1508–9, of the *Rhetoric* in the original Greek, as part of the *Rhetores Graeci,* in which appeared also the *Poetics* and certain portions of Dionysius.[9] In 1553 was published the *Arte of Rhetorique* of Thomas Wilson, who had entered King's College, Cambridge, as a scholar from Eton, in 1541. Through Cicero and Quintilian, if not directly, Wilson's *Rhetorique* goes back to Aristotle. Wilson had the good fortune to be at King's College when Sir John Cheke was Provost; and he shared with the Provost not only the love of Greek but a dislike for those cumbrous Latinisms which were driving out many neater native expressions and

thus spoiling the simplicity and raciness of English speech. If the study of ancient rhetoric
helped Cheke and Wilson in this, it surely did a
good day's work.[10] It should be added that,
when Milton in his *Tractate* couples together
Aristotle and 'Phalereus,' he is thinking of
Demetrius of Phalerum, a pupil of Theophrastus, and of the treatise on *Style* then attributed
to this Demetrius who flourished about 300 B.C.
Elsewhere we have given reasons for assigning
the treatise to the first century A.D., and for
conjecturing that the author is that Demetrius
in Plutarch who had been in Britain and was
probably the dedicator of the two Greek votive
tablets now preserved in the Museum at York.
Whatever its date and authorship may have
been, the treatise on *Style* was long a text-book
of speech and writing and literary taste in the
universities of modern Europe and was known
not only to Milton but to Coleridge and (in our
own day) to the two authors of *English Lessons
for English People.*[11]

Greek Literary Criticism suffered from its
close association with Greek Rhetoric. Longinus, with his intense love of literature for its
own sake, revolted against this bondage. He
had the advantage, over Aristotle, of living at a

time when he could compare one literature with another. He can also find in literature the re-flexion of national, as well as individual, life. But it is Aristotle who, in his *Poetics* and his *Rhetoric,* endeavours to cover the whole field of literary criticism and rhetoric as these studies presented themselves in his day; and, notwith-standing the great differences between the ancient and the modern languages, a recent book on *Ancient Rhetoric and Poetic* [12] sees in Aristotle a true guide to modern 'composition' in its broadest sense, as well as an unsurpassed critic. In regard to the appreciation and the practice of prose-writing in particular, much may still be learnt from the ancient conception (too often ignored to-day) of prose as an art and an art closely related to that of poetry; from the stress laid on good taste, variety, and euphony; from the respect paid to *hellenismus,* or the use of Pure Greek. Pure Greek suggests an ideal of Pure English for the great 'Common Dialect' of the modern English-speaking world.[13] And for every student of the ancient Greek world, the theory and practice of Greek speaking and writing, *as viewed by the Greeks themselves,* must always have a special interest and value.

[150]

NOTES

⁎ For certain abbreviations used in the Notes, see below page 163

I **1.** Plat., *Gorg.*, 453 A: a definition variously attributed to (1) Corax and Tisias, or to (2) Isocrates. **2.** Plat., *Phaedr.*, 230 ff., 266–269. **3.** *ib.* 260 ff. **4.** *ib.* 261 A, 271 C. **5.** Plat., *Politicus*, 303, 4: contrast *Laws*, 937, 8. **6.** Plat., *Phaedr.*, 268. **7.** *ib.* 245 ff., 277; *Symp.*, 196 D. **8.** *Phaedr.*, 264 C: cp. Arist., *Poet.*, 1450 b 34–36. **9.** Plat., *Laws*, 659. **10.** Plat., *Rep.*, iii. 393 E: for the deliberate *prosification* of Homer cp. 381 A. **11.** Cic., *De Orat.* I. 47: tr. E. N. P. Moor. **12.** Like Thucydides in his Speeches, Plato would "keep as close as possible to the general tenour of what was actually said" (Thucyd. i. c. 22). **13.** Dionysius Halic., *Demosth.*, c. 23. **14.** Milton, *De Idea Platonica*. **15.** Plat., *Ion*, 531 ff. **16.** Plat., *Rep.*, 401 C. **17.** Cp. "*C. V.*," pp. 264–7, as to the opening words of the *Republic* itself. **18.** E.g., *Rep.*, 595 C, *Phaedr.* 245 A. **19.** Cp. Lane Cooper, *Aristotelian Theory of Comedy*, New York, 1922, p. 103. **20.** Plat., *Protag.*, 337. **21.** *Gorg.*, 448 C: perhaps a quotation. **22.** *Symp.*, 195–7. **23.** *ib.* 223. **24.** In the earliest and the latest of his extant plays Aristophanes attacks the *rhetors*, but not on literary grounds: cp. *Ach.*, 38, 680, *Plut.*, 30, 379, 567. **25.** "Quotation and Parody in Shakespeare" would be a good subject for an academic dissertation. **26.** Aristoph., *Frogs*, 88 ff.; *Birds*, 904–958; *Wasps*, 57 ff. **27.** Aristotle, *Poetics*, 1451 b 21: tr. Butcher. Or, 'Agathon's *Antheus*.' **28.** Cp. W. Rhys Roberts, "Aristophanes and Agathon," in *The Journal of Hellenic Studies*, XX, 44–56 (1900): a paper from which some sentences are here taken. J. D. Denniston, *Greek Literary Criticism*, London and New York, 1924 (in "The Library of Greek Thought" Series), p. xii, calls attention to new terms of criticism in the *Frogs*: as also in his article "Technical Terms

[153]

in Aristophanes," in *The Classical Quarterly*, XXI, 113–121 (1927). For literary criticism in Greek comedy generally, see various passages in Pickard-Cambridge's *Greek Comic Fragments*, and cf. Saintsbury's *Loci Critici*, p. 32 (Simylus).

II **1.** Roberts, "References to Plato in Aristotle's *Rhetoric*," in *Classical Philology*, XIX, 342–6 (1924). **2.** *Rhet.*, I. c. 1; cf. "Notes on Aristotle's *Rhetoric*," in *The American Journal of Philology*, XLV, 351–361 (1924). **3.** *ib.* I. c. 2. **4.** *Eth. Nic.*, 1094 b 25. **5.** *Rhet.*, 1355 a 4 ff. **6.** *ib.* I. c. 2. **7.** *ib.* 1356 a 25. **8.** *ib.* 1359 b 9. **9.** *Rhet.*, I. c. 3. **10.** *ib.* I. cc. 4–8. **11.** *ib.* I. c. 9. **12.** *ib.* I. cc. 10–15. **13.** *ib.* II. c. 1. **14.** *ib.* II. cc. 2–11. **15.** *ib.* II. cc. 12–14. **16.** *ib.* II, cc. 15–17. **17.** *ib.* II. cc. 18–26. **18.** Cp. such passages as the following in Roberts' Translation of the *Rhetoric*: 1359 b 19–1360 a 37, 1361 a 5–11, 1381 b 1–9, 1381 b 28–32, 1389 a 2–1390 b 12 (this description of Youth and Age will, like Bacon's, never lose its interest), 1390 b 25–31, 1391 a 13–18. **19.** Compare *Rhet.*, 1354 a 6–11, with *Gorg.*, 463 B and 501 A. **20.** *Gorg.*, 453 A, E: cf. p. 153 above. **21.** *Soph.El.*, 183 b 29 ff., *Pol.* 1305 a 12. **22.** *Eth.N.*, 1094 b 3; cf. Plat. *Euthyd.*, 307 A. **23.** *Rhet.*, 1410 b 3. **24.** Roberts, "The New Rhetorical Fragment (*Oxyrhynchus Papyri*, Part iii, pp. 27–30) in relation to the Sicilian Rhetoric of Corax and Tisias," in *The Classical Review*, XVIII, 18–21 (1904). **25.** Walz, *Rhetores Graeci*, iv. 13, V. 215. **26.** *Rhet.*, 1354 b 28; *Theaet.*, 172 ff., and *Laws*, 938. **27.** Diog. L., viii. 57. **28.** *Rhet.*, 1404 a 24–29. **29.** Dionys. Hal., *de Imit.*, ii. 8. **30.** For oratory of all kinds, admirable patterns are to be found in *Iliad*, I and IX, and throughout Homer. **31.** Diod. Sic., xii. 53. **32.** The best Greek and Latin taste, oratorical and literary, prose and verse, was always on its guard against the too numerous rhymes presented by the inflected forms in the two languages. **33.** Cp. " *C. Demetr.*," p. 4, and *The Classical Review*, XVIII. p. 19 (article mentioned in note 24, above). **34.** Shakespeare, *King Henry IV*, Pt. I, Act 2, Sc. 4. **35.** *Rhet.*, iii. c. 3. **36.** *Gorg.*, 520 A. **37.** Xen., *Mem.*, i. 6, 13; *Anab.*, ii. 6, 16. **38.** *Soph.El.*, 165 a 22. **39.** *Rhet.*, i. 1 fin. **40.** For an excellent translation, by E. S. Forster, of the *Rhet. ad Al.*, see

VOL. XI of the Oxford Translation of Aristotle. **41.** *Rhet. ad Al.*, 1432 a 7–10, tr. Forster. **42.** Isocr., *Panath.*, 117, 118. A much needed modern version of Isocrates is about to appear in *The Loeb Library*, from the hand of George Norlin. **43.** Isocr., *Philipp.*, 12. **44.** Isocr., *Antid.*, 271, *c. Soph.* 8, *Hel. Enc.* 5. **45.** Plat., *Gorg.*, 463 A: a parody apparently of *c. Soph.* 17. **46.** Plat., *Euthyd.*, 304–6. **47.** Plat., *Phaedr.*, 279. **48.** Isocr., *Panath.*, 30–32. **49.** Aristotle, and certain of the Attic Orators, quote the Greek poets freely: not so Isocrates. **50.** Arist., *Rhet.*, 1407 a 6. **51.** *ib.* 1401 b 34. **52.** Diog. L., *Arist.*, c. 4. **53.** Strabo, *Geogr.*, 618: cf. Roberts, in *The Classical Review*, XXXIX, 176 (1925). **54.** Plut., *Alex.*, c. 7.

III **1.** Arist., *Polit.*, 1281 b 7: tr. Jowett-Davis. **2.** Id. *Poet.*, c. 22. **3.** Id. *Rhet.*, 1404 a 12. **4.** *ib.* 1404 a 24ff. **5.** *ib.* 1413 b 3ff. **6.** Plat., *Phaedr.*, 274, 275. **7.** Translated by LaRue Van Hook, in *The Classical Weekly*, XII, 89–94 (1919), "On the Writers of Written Discourses." **8.** The same Alcidamas is censured by Aristotle for describing the *Odyssey* as "a goodly looking-glass of human life," *Rhet.*, 1406 b 12. **9.** *Cf.* Roberts, "Aristotle on Public Speaking," in *The Fortnightly Review*, CXVI, 201–210, p. 205 (August, 1924). **10.** *Rhet.*, 1414 a 19 ff. **11.** *Demetrius on Style:* in *The Loeb Classical Library*, 1927; pp. 270–278. **12.** Quint., IV. 2, 63. **13.** "*L.Demetr.*," pp. 261, 327. **14.** Cf. G. L. Hendrickson's two able articles, in *The American Journal of Philology*, XXV, 125–146, XXVI, 249–290 (1904 and 1905), on the Ancient Characters of Style. **15.** *Rhet.*, iii. c. 9. **16.** "*L.Demetr.*," pp. 307–9. Winckelmann quotes the passage in his *Geschichte der Kunst des Alterthums*, p. 240, ed 1764. For similar references to art-analogies, cp. Dionys. Halic., *De Isocr.*, c. 3, *De Isaeo*, c. 4, *De Dinarcho*, c. 7. Cicero and Quintilian also, in writing of oratory, often draw illustrations from the plastic and graphic arts. **17.** "*L.Demetr.*," p. 309. **18.** *ib.* p. 325. **19.** E.g. *ib.* pp. 365, 371. **20.** *ib.* p. 439. **21.** *ib.* p. 409. **22.** See the summaries in "*C.Demetr.*," pp. 28–34 and "*L.Demetr.*," pp. 290–293. The four types of style are the *elevated*, the *elegant*, the *plain*, and the *forcible* and the qualities of each are fully discussed. The modern literary illustrations given in both editions will help to show that Demetrius' principles are of universal application. **23.** *"L.Demetr.,"* p. 439. **24.** *ib.* pp. 441, 443. **25.** *ib.* p. 321. **26.** *ib.* p. 353. **27.** *ib.* p. 373. **28.** Plutarch, *Mor.*, 79 B. **29.** *"L.Demetr.,"* pp. 373–381, 417, 449, 487. According to Anatole France, the vice of 'écrire trop bien' is the worst of all. **30.** *ib.* p. 455. **31.** *ib.* pp. 469, 465. **32.** *ib.* pp. 432–5. **33.** Plat., *Phaedr.*, 260 E, 262 B. **34.** *"L.Demetr.,"* pp. 317, 437. **35.** Aesch., *Fragm.*, 176: cp. Eur., *Phoen.*, 469. **36.** Arist., *Rhet.*, iii. c. 2. **37.** Homer, *Il.*, xiv. 301; cp. Plut., *Def. Or.*, c. 2.

IV **1.** Quintil., iii. 1, 16; ix. 3, 89; ix. 4, 88. See also Roberts' "Caecilius of Calacte: a contribution to the history of Greek Literary Criticism," in *The American Journal of Philology*, XVIII, 302–312 (1897). **2.** If Aristotle had really done anything to train Demosthenes (instead of Alexander), it would have been through his earlier and more directly practical writings on rhetoric now lost, such as the *Gryllus*, the *Theodectea*, and one or another τέχνη, *technē* (*manual of rhetoric*) ascribed to him in Diogenes Laertius and elsewhere. These writings were no doubt *exoteric* or pamphlets meant for the general public, while our *Rhetoric* would be *acroamatic* or lecture-notes designed for select hearers possessed of some philosophical aptitude. **3.** "D.H.," *Essay on Deinarchus*, c.9. **4.** *Ep. ad Amm.*, I. c. 2. **5.** See further *"D.H.,"* pp. 38–43; H. P. Breitenbach, *The 'De Compositione' of Dionysius of Halicarnassus considered with reference to the 'Rhetoric' of Aristotle;* G. Ammon, *De Dionysii Halicarnassensis Rhetoricorum Fontibus*, Munich, 1889. **6.** *"C.Demetr.,"* p. 8. In connexion with Isocrates and his influence, see Roberts, "Theopompus in the Greek Literary Critics: with special reference to the newly-discovered Greek historian," in *The Classical Review*, XXII, 118–122 (1908). **7.** *"D.H.,"* p. 22. **8.** *"D.H.,"* pp. 24, 25 (for details). **9.** *"D.H.,"* p. 5. n. 1. **10.** Thucyd., vii. 69–72; iii. 81, 82. **11.** Cic., *Or.* 32. **12.** *"D.H.,"* *de Thucyd.*, c. 51. **13.** Thucyd., I. c. 23. **14.** *"D.H.,"* p. 137. **15.** *"C.V.,"* p. 183. **16.** *Rhet.*, 1415 b 31; cf. 1367 b 8. **17.** *"C.V.,"* p. 31: Boileau, Malherbe. **18.** *ib.* p. 200 l. 18. **19.** *ib.* pp. 160 l. 23, 228 l. 9. **20.** *ib.* p. 251. **21.** *ib.*

p. 267. **22.** *ib.* pp. 123–5. **23.** *Rhet.*, 1408 b 21–32.
24. "*C.V.*," p. 254. **25.** "*C. Demetr.*," p. 10. **26.** "*C.V.*,"
p. 254. **27.** Cic., *Or.*, § 67; *De Or.*, iii. § 184. **28.** "*C.V.*,"
pp. 193–199. **29.** *ib.* pp. 133–135. **30.** *ib.* p. 244.
31. "*D.H.*," p. 47. **32.** "*C.V.*," p. 79. **33.** Hom., *Od.*,
vi. 57. **34.** Hom., *Il.*, xviii. 386. **35.** Cic., *ad Att.*, xii. 6.
36. In Dionysius we find anticipations of literary phrases
which we may think particularly modern; for example, 'hackneyed,' 'enjambement,' 'the style is the man,' 'with the eye
on the object.' — The extent, variety, and excellence of the
critical remains of Dionysius, and the comparative neglect
into which they have fallen, have called for a somewhat detailed treatment in this chapter.

V **1.** Cf. the wide sense sometimes borne by 'eloquentia'
in Latin and 'eloquence' in English. With the ancient
Greeks, even "to read" commonly meant "to read *aloud*."
2. *Rhet.*, 1398 b 15. **3.** Plat., *Apol.*, 26 D. **4.** *Rhet.*,
1413 b 4; cf. p. 54 above. **5.** Quintil., ii. 1, 4. **6.** The names
and approximate dates of the first four Librarians of Alexandria are: (1) Zenodotus, 285–234 B.C.; (2) Eratosthenes,
234–195; (3) Aristophanes of Byzantium, 195–180; (4) Aristarchus, 180–146. (Between (1) and (2) may have come Callimachus; between (2) and (3) Apollonius of Rhodes.) The
Alexandrian age may be regarded as covering the three centuries from 300–1 B.C. Alexandria itself was founded in 331
B.C. **7.** "*L.Demetr.*," pp. 421–3. **8.** Plut., *Vit. Demosth.*, c. 5.
9. Thucyd., i. c. 126. **10.** The lion, it seems, had forgotten
to be leonine; or should we rather say 'Leontine' (like Gor-
gias)? **11.** Strab., *Geogr.*, I. 1, 10. **12.** *ib.* I. 2, 15. **13.** *ib.*
XIII. 2, 3. — For references to Sappho in ancient Greek writers
see J. M. Edmonds, *Lyra Graeca*, in *The Loeb Classical Library*,
London and New York, 1922–24, I. pp. 140–307; and consult
chapters i and vi in D.M. Robinson's *Sappho and her Influence.*
The latter volume, appearing in *this Series*, is a valuable and
uniquely comprehensive study of Sappho, in the light of
ancient and modern literature and art. **14.** Strab., *Geogr.*, I.
2, 6: cf. *The Geography of Strabo*, transl. by H. L. Jones, in *The
Loeb Classical Library*, London and New York, 1917–1927 (4
vols. have appeared). **15.** *Anth. Pal.*, vii. 718. **16.** Athen.,

Deipnos., xiii. 596 B. **17.** J. W. Mackail, *Select Epigrams from the Greek Anthology*, London and New York, 1906, p. 179 and p. 50. **18.** Cf. p. 50 above. **19.** Dio Chrys., *Or.*, 53, 1. **20.** Dio Chrys., *Or.*, 52. Cf. Roberts, *The Contemporary Review*, CXXIX April, 1926, pp. 482–489, "Ulysses in Greek Tragedy." **21.** St. John Chrysostom, *De Sacerdotio*, iv. 6: J. A. Nairn's edition, Cambridge, 1906, p. 120. **22.** As translated by G. W. Butterworth, *Clement of Alexandria*, in *The Loeb Classical Library*, London and New York, 1919, p. 213. **23.** Emerson, in his introduction to W. W. Goodwin's *Revised Translation of Plutarch's Morals*, I. p. xi. **24.** Plut., *Mor.*, 79; briefly discussed, from one aspect, by Roberts in *The Classical Review*, XL, 115, (1926). Cf. pp. 65–66 above. **25.** Plut., *How to Listen*, §14. **26.** Plut., *De Prof. in Virt.*, § 8. For Plutarch, under various aspects, see Roberts' *Ancient Boeotians*, Cambridge, England, 1895, p. 91 (Index). **27.** *Epictetus, The Discourses and the Manual*, iii. 5, 10; tr. P. E. Matheson, Oxford, 1916 (2 vols.). **28.** *Marc. Aur.*, i. 7; tr., Rendall. **29.** *Marcus Aurelius*, xi. 6; tr. G. H. Rendall, London and New York, 1898 (2d ed.). **30.** Galen, *De Facultatibus Naturalibus*, c. 1. **30a.** Cf. F. G. Allinson's *Lucian* (appearing in this Series). **31.** Lucian, *De Conscr. Hist.*, §§ 41–43 (tr. Fowler, or Harmon). **32.** See C. S. Baldwin's paper on "St. Augustine and the Rhetoric of Cicero," in *Classical Association Proceedings*, XXII, 24–46 (1925). **32a.** For Aristeides, see E. D. T. Jenkins (reviewing Schmid's new Teubner text) in the *Classical Review*, XLI (1927), p. 200. **33.** Julianus, *contra Galilaeos*, 131 C; tr. W. C. Wright, Vol. III of *The Works of The Emperor Julian*, in *The Loeb Classical Library*, London and New York, 1923. **34.** For Ausonius (who occasionally wrote in Greek) reference may be made to (1) H. G. Evelyn White's *Ausonius* I and II ("Loeb" Series), (2), E. K. Rand's paper, "Ausonius, the First French Poet," in *Classical Association Proceedings*, XXIV, 28–41 (1927). — Greek literary criticism found in the Patriarch Photius, as late as the ninth century A.D., has been studied by LaRue Van Hook, and by Emil Orth. — Reference may also be made to H. M. Hubbell's paper on "The *Rhetorica* of Philodemus," in *Transactions of the Connecticut Academy*, XXIII, 243–382 (1920).

VI **1.** Cf. Roberts' paper in *Classical Association Proceedings*, XXV (Apr., 1928). The likeliest period seems to be 25–50 A.D. For the historical Longinus, see "Long.", pp. 35, 245–6. **2.** Perhaps there is no nearer Greek equivalent for 'literary criticism' than that found in *De Subl.*, c. vi: cf. *"Long.,"* p. 211 (summary of c. vi). **3.** *"Long.,"* p. 95. **4.** *ib.* p. 121. **5.** *ib.* pp. 91–117. **6.** *ib.* p. 119. **7.** *ib.* pp. 119–127. **8.** *ib.* pp. 127–133. **9.** *ib.* pp. 133–135. **10.** *ib.* pp. 135–137. **11.** *ib.* pp. 139–141. **12.** *ib.* pp. 141ff. **13.** Cf. *"Long.,"* pp. 12–15. **14.** *ib.* p. 57.

VII **1.** *"Long.,"* p. 79; Plat., *Rep.*, ix. 586 A. **2.** Dante, *Inferno*, xxvi. 119. **3.** With Milton's 'lowly' we may compare *Rhet. ad. Her.*, IV. 8, 11, 'attenuata est, quae *demissa* est usque ad usitatissimam puri consuetudinem sermonis.' — Whether, in the Greek text of *Subl.*, c. 2 init., the word βάθος is genuine and means what we now understand by it, or whether we owe the useful English term 'bathos' to Alexander Pope, is a difficult question still awaiting solution. Βάθος occurs nowhere else in the essay, which uses various other words to express the same general notion of a fall from the sublime to the ridiculous; and although the revised 'Liddell & Scott' translates it, in this passage, by 'bathos,' no other example of the usage is offered. **4.** In Cicero's rhetorical writings, *elatus* and related words may possibly be used instead of *sublimis*. With the complete line in Chaucer's *Clerk's Prologue* (l. 18) we might compare Demetrius § 234 and an English sentence which was written in the year 1595 and is quoted in Murray's *New English Dictionary* under the word 'sublime'. The reference, in each of these three passages, to *letter-writing* and to *kings* is noteworthy. **5.** The work is, however, mentioned on p. 212 of Conrad Gesner's *Bibliotheca Universalis*, which was published in 1545: a reference kindly supplied to me (in 1901) by Mr. Donald S. Robertson. **6.** Cp. A. Rosenberg, *Longinus in England bis zum Ende des 18 Jahrhunderts*, Berlin, 1917. **7.** *"C.V.,"* p. 203; *"L.Demetr."* p. 348. The years in which Dionysius' critical works were successively printed are given [under the names of Aldus, Stephanus, and Sylburg] in *"D.H.,"* pp. 209, 210. A valuable Isocratean study is H. M. Hubbell's "The Influence of Isocrates on Cicero, Dionysius and Aristides": New Haven, Yale University Press, 1913. **8.** Details in A. W. T. Stahr's *Aristoteles bei den Römern*, Leipzig, 1834. **9.** For the period before the printing of the Greek text of the *Rhetoric*, see M. T. Herrick's excellent paper on "The Early History of Aristotle's *Rhetoric* in England," in the *Philological Quarterly*, V, 242–257 (1926). Mr. Herrick discusses Aristotle's influence on Thomas Wilson (*Arte of Rhetorique*, 1553, 1560), Ascham (1560), Sir Philip Sidney (1577), Francis Bacon, Theodore Goulston (1619) and concludes that for the 17th and 18th centuries Aristotle was the "veritable dictator in literary criticism." In a letter to me, Mr. Herrick points out that Giraldus Cambrensis (c. 1146–1220 A.D.) seems to mean *Rhet.* 1355 b 10–13 in Giraldus' *De Invectionibus*, Part V, c. 4: "Unde et Aristoteles: 'Nec medicus semper sanabit nec orator semper persuadebit; sed si ex contingentibus nil omiserunt, satis utramque propositum dicemus habere disciplinam.'" Giraldus may here be drawing on his rhetorical training in theUniversity of Paris, whose earliest statute (at the beginning of the thirteenth century) insists on the study of Plato and Aristotle. The existing *Vetusta* (the old Latin translation of the *Rhetoric* by William of Moerbeke) did not appear till some fifty years after his death, but there had been Latin versions earlier in the thirteenth century. **10.** Cf. G. H. Mair's edition, Oxford, 1909, of Thomas Wilson's book, *Arte of Rhetorique* (1560). The influence of Greek and Latin rhetoric and criticism is illustrated by such books as Ascham's *Schoolmaster*, Brinsley's *Ludus Literarius*, Hoole's *New Discovery of Old Art of Teaching School*, Farnaby's *Index Rhetoricus*, and (among modern books) Foster Watson's *The English Grammar Schools to 1660*, D. L. Clark's *Rhetoric and Poetry in the Renaissance*, and Spingarn's *Literary Criticism in the Renaissance* and *Critical Essays of the Seventeenth Century*. There is an excellent chapter on "Boileau, Longinus, and 'The Sublime'" in A. F. B. Clark's *Boileau and the French Classical Critics in England (1660–1830)*, Paris, 1925. **11.** Cf. "*L.Demetr.*," pp. 270–278; 281, 282. "In the year 1871 two classical graduates of Cambridge, who were also excellent writers of English and workers distinguished in many lines of activity, E. A. Abbott and J. R.

Seeley, brought out their *English Lessons for English People*
. . . They find it convenient to apply the terms *simple,*
elevated, graceful, and *forcible,* to the characteristic styles of
various English poets — Wordsworth, Milton, Tennyson,
Shakespeare." **12.** *Ancient Rhetoric and Poetic,* interpreted
from representative works, by Charles Sears Baldwin, New
York, 1924. **13.** For the Greek language and its chequered
history, cf. A. Meillet, *Aperçu d'une histoire de la langue*
grecque, Paris, 1913; for modern English, the publications of
The Society for Pure English.

BIBLIOGRAPHY

The modern writings on Greek Rhetoric and Literary Criticism are numberless. Some of them will be suggested by such names as: Ammon, Arnim, Aulitzky; Baldwin, Blass, Bosanquet, Breitenbach, Brzoska, Butcher, Bywater; Caplan, Chaignet, Clark, Cooper, Cope, Croiset; Denniston, Diels, Drerup; Egger, Ernesti; Fuhr; Gayley, Gildersleeve, Gomperz, Goodell, Grote, Gummere; Hammer, Hannah, Hendrickson, Herrick, Van Hook, Hubbell, Hunt; Immisch; Jahn, Janzon, Jebb; Kaibel, Kroll, Kuiper; Laurand, Lebègue, Lehnert; Mutschmann; Nassal, Navarre, Norden; Orth; Photiades, Prickard; Radermacher, Rolfe; Saintsbury, Sandys, Scott, Shorey, Spengel, Spingarn, Stroux, Süss; Twining, Tyrwhitt; Usener; Vahlen, Vaucher, Volkmann; Walz, Watson (Foster), Welldon, Wendland, Wichelns, Wilamowitz. Fuller bibliographical details will be found in Roberts' editions as follows:

Dionysius of Halicarnassus: The Three Literary Letters, Greek Text, English Translation, Notes, etc. Cambridge, England, 1901. "D. H."

Dionysius of Halicarnassus: On Literary Composition, Greek Text, Translation, Notes, etc. London and New York, 1910. "C. V."

Longinus on the Sublime, Greek Text, Translation, Notes, etc. Cambridge, England, second edition, 1907. "Long."

Demetrius: On Style, Greek Text, Translation, Notes, etc. Cambridge, England, 1902. "C. Demetr."

Demetrius: On Style, in *The Loeb Classical Library.* Greek Text, Translation, Notes, etc. London and New York, 1927. "L. Demetr."

These editions are cited in the *Notes* by the abbreviations given above, and Roberts' Oxford *Translation of Aristotle's Rhetoric* (1924), by the abbreviation "Rhet."

[163]

BIBLIOGRAPHY

The following are the full titles of some modern books in which the history of Greek Rhetoric and Literary Criticism is traced: —

BALDWIN, C. S., *Ancient Rhetoric and Poetic*. New York, 1924.

DENNISTON, J. D., *Greek Literary Criticism*. London and New York, 1924 (appearing in " The Library of Greek Thought " Series).

EGGER, Émile, *Essai sur l'Histoire de la Critique chez les Grecs*.[2] Paris, 1885.

SAINTSBURY, G., *A History of Criticism*. Edinburgh and London, 1900.

SANDYS, J. E., *A History of Classical Scholarship*. Cambridge, England, 1903.

Reference should also be made to:

BLASS, F., *Attische Beredsamkeit*. Leipzig, 1887.

JEBB, R. C., *Attic Orators*. London and New York, 1876.

NORDEN, E., *Antike Kunstprosa*. Leipzig, 1898.

VOLKMANN-HAMMER, *Rhetorik und Metrik der Griechen und Römer*. Munich, 1901.